SPIRITUAL UPGRADE

CHALLENGING YOURSELF TO IMPROVE

VAN I. SHARPE

Copyright © 2009 by Van I. Sharpe

Spiritual Upgrade
Challenging Yourself To Improve
by Van I. Sharpe

Printed in the United States of America

ISBN 978-1-60791-744-1

All rights reserved solely by the author. The author guarantees all contents are original and do not infringe upon the legal rights of any other person or work. No part of this book may be reproduced in any form without the permission of the author. The views expressed in this book are not necessarily those of the publisher.

Unless otherwise indicated, Bible quotations are taken from The Authorized King James Version, Copyright © 2000 by The Zondervan Corporation, and The Amplified Bible, Copyright © 1954, 1958, 1964, 1965, 1987 by The Lockman Foundation, and The Message: The Bible in Contemporary Language, Copyright © 2002 by Eugene H. Peterson, and The Living Bible, Copyright © 1971 by Tyndale House Publishers, Wheaton, Illinois, and The New International Version of the Bible, Copyright © 1973, 1978, 1984 by International Bible Society.

Back cover photograph of the author by Solomon's Photography
(252) 641-0054

Bishop Van I. Sharpe
Newness of Life Christian Center
P. O. Box 1462
Tarboro, N.C. 27886
(252) 641-0098
Fax: (252) 823-7110
E-mail: reesiesharpe@embarqmail.com

www.xulonpress.com

In memory of my little brother,
Myron Lee Sharpe, whose love and smile
I miss dearly.

ABOUT THE AUTHOR

Bishop Van I. Sharpe is a resident and native of Tarboro, N.C. He is a graduate from Tarboro High School in Tarboro and graduated Magna Cum Laude with a B.A. degree in Mass Communications from Shaw University in Raleigh, N.C. While attending Shaw University, he was an honor student and a member of various honor societies including: Who's Who Among College Students, Alpha Chi National Honor Society, Alpha Chi National Honor Society, Alpha Epsilon Rho Honor Society, and National Dean's List.

Bishop Van I. Sharpe is the pastor and founder of Newness of Life Christian Center in Tarboro, N.C. He is married to Resunester Sharpe, and they are the proud parents of one lovely daughter, Vanneika Aireesh Sharpe. His ministry includes pastoring, developing and fortifying leaders, flowing in the prophetic, and evangelizing in various states.

CONTENTS

ACKNOWLEDGEMENTS xiii

INTRODUCTION xv

SLOWLY, BUT SURELY 17

YOU'RE TOO BLESSED TO BE OFFENDED ... 21

SPIRITUAL UPGRADE 23

WHAT DOES GOD USE TO UPGRADE US SPIRITUALLY 25

CHARACTER TRAITS OF A LIVING EXAMPLE *31*

UPGRADING OUR PRAYER LIFE 35

EIGHT THINGS TO KNOW ABOUT PRAYER *39*

FIVE THINGS WE MUST BE IN PRAYER 45

UPGRADING OUR COMMITMENT 49

THREE THINGS YOUR COMMITMENT WILL ATTRACT 57

THREE THINGS WE MUST BE IN ORDER TO UPGRADE OUR COMMITMENT 59

WHY AREN'T PEOPLE COMMITED TO GOD AND HIS KINGDOM? 63

UPGRADING OUR OPEN DOOR 69

THINGS WE MUST DO TO UPGRADE OUR OPEN DOOR 81

UPGRADING YOURSELF IN THE PRESENCE OF GOD 89

THREE WAYS TO COME INTO GOD'S PRESENCE 97

WHAT DOES THE PRESENCE OF GOD DO FOR US? 103

UGRADING YOUR SPIRITUAL SENSITIVITY 119
(CHECKING YOUR SPIRITUAL REFLEXES)

UPGRADING YOUR HEALTH AND RELATIONSHIPS 123

UPGRADING YOUR FOCUS 135

UPGRADING YOURSELF IN EXCELLENCE ... 139

UPGRADING THROUGH THE TRUMPET 149

EPILOGUE (CHALLENGE YOURSELF) 153

ACKNOWLEDGMENTS

I am very appreciative towards the chosen believers of one of the greatest churches in Eastern N. C. at Newness of Life Christian Center in Tarboro, N.C., whose love, faithfulness, prayers and steadfast endurance inspire me to reach for new heights in the kingdom of God. Thanks a million!

My precious wife, Resunester, who is indeed the help suitable for me to operate in dominion in the earth. Your spirit toward the kingdom is as beautiful as your name. I love you very much!

My daughter, Vanneika, your potential is astronomical. Thank you for the privilege I have of speaking into your life. Keep striving for excellence.

My mother, a woman of great wisdom, who is always seeking to do nice things for people. I love you Mom.

Special thanks to my sisters, Susan and Gloria, who continue to look better with age. Pastor Susan thanks for being a light to me when I was in darkness.

My brother, Pastor Wayne, whose prayer life continues to inspire me, and his wife, Marjorie, who always seems to say the right thing at the right time.

Bishop Marvin Smith, whose fathering and instructions motivated me to do the impossible. I honor you in the kingdom.

Deacon Anthony Solomon it looks like you've done it again. Thanks for being such an awesome photographer.

Special thanks to Beverly Reynolds whose patience and smile in proofreading this book made writing it such a delight. I'm glad you're married to my brother-in-law, Frankie Reynolds.

Thank you **Minnie Dickens** of AJ's Barber Shop (252) 212-3941 and **Marlow Brinson** of Royal Kutz (252) 641-4774 for your great barber skills.

Much love to every anointed man and woman of God who have prayed for me and the vision the Lord has put in my heart.

INTRODUCTION

The ability to make progress is the burning desire of leaders who understand that moving backwards is not an option. We must always seek to improve and rise to new plateaus in the Lord Jesus Christ. I can recall many years ago the words of my armor bearer, Kenwin Alleyne. He stated four potent words to me as he joined our local church, "Forward ever, Backwards never." Kenwin was from the island of Trinidad, and I could see the sincerity in his eyes and hunger in his heart for truth. Before he joined our church, he would come up to me and say, "Sharp preacher, sharp dresser, but dirty car." Notice the first two things were compliments, but the last thing was not. I remember smiling at him and walking away. The next Sunday after the service was over, he approached me again and uttered the exact same words, "Sharp preacher, sharp dresser, but dirty car." I was thinking in my mind who is this guy and why does he keep saying something to me about my car. The next Sunday came and we had a powerful move of the Spirit and guess who came up to me; yes you got it, Kenwin! He repeated this phrase the third time, "Sharp preacher, sharp dresser, but dirty car." By now I had heard enough, so I asked him what did he want me to do about it? He replied, "I'll take care of it. I'll clean it for you." He told me that he had details skills, and he had noticed my car wasn't as clean as it should have been. His desire was to see me be a sharp preacher, sharp dresser, and have a sharp car. I was all for it. I had been so busy traveling, counseling and helping others that I hadn't taken the time to wash my car or take it to the car wash. My wife had mentioned to me that I needed to do something about it, but I was too busy helping others. Not to mention that by the time I would finish preaching and teaching the word, I would be too tired to wash it. Yet, God in his wisdom and mercy had sent brother Kenwin to assist me (Thank you Jesus)! He's been taking care of my cars ever since.

Sometimes God, who knows and understands the busyness of your day will send someone into your life to challenge you to upgrade an area that ultimately will cause everything else in your life to look bad. The same way God used Kenwin to point out an area that was taking away from who I was ordained to be, I pray that this book will do the same for you. Kenwin helped me to upgrade myself by addressing this area because he cared and had thought out a solution. I can boldly say that I care about those whom my heavenly Father allowed Jesus Christ to die for. I care enough to offer you spiritual insights in order to upgrade your life. These insights will allow you to move, "Forward ever and Backwards never!"

SLOWLY, BUT SURELY

"I am a slow walker, but I never walk back."
Abraham Lincoln (16th President)

This statement made by one of our nation's greatest President speaks to the fact that the goal should be to go forward and never backward. It also alludes to the fact that we shouldn't worry about how fast we are going as long as it's toward the goal we have set for ourselves. Many times we allow the devil to cheat or rob us of the joy we are about to lay hold of because we worry about how long it takes. This causes us to rush ourselves and become impatient with ourselves and others.

This statement made by one of our former President's brings back to my remembrance a statement that my dad use to quote frequently. He would always say, "Slowly but surely." He would always tell my brother and I these words when we would go somewhere with him, and we wanted to leave immediately or in a hurry. My dad would tell us that he was coming, slowly but surely. This meant that he wasn't moving as fast as we would have liked him to, but he was coming. He was moving at his own pace.

It is important that you and I know our pace in the kingdom of God. We must walk at the pace the Holy Spirit is leading us. We walk at this pace with total assurance that the Lord will never lead us backward or at a pace which is too fast for us to keep up with him. Others may beat you there and think that you will never arrive, but the truth of the matter is that you are coming. You are not as swift and fast as they are and they have arrived to their destination first, yet God is bringing you right along.

This would irritate my brother and I so bad. We would resent that we were with our father. He would tell us that he was coming, and we would have to wait another thirty five or forty minutes. He would talk to someone else and we would still find ourselves waiting. Eventually he would leave and we would leave with him, but my brother and I would be upset. We wouldn't tell daddy because we knew he would be angry at us for trying to rush him. Yet, we couldn't understand why he wanted to go over to some friend's house and talk all day about stuff that seemed so insignificant.

One of the things that the statement made by Abraham Lincoln is also revealing to us is that as you get older your pace slows down. His steps weren't strong and powerful like they were in his younger years, but they were still in the right direction. Sometimes young people get so concerned about the pace that we fail to pay attention to direction. God is more concerned about direction than he is the pace.

Your steps are not quite as fast, but you are on your way. You are headed in the right direction.

> "Efforts and courage are not enough without purpose and direction."
> **John F. Kennedy** (35th President)

Many believers fail to understand that the steps you make as you get older must be more purposeful. They are done with destiny in mind because you understand the serious consequences associated with bad decisions. You don't have as much time as you used to. You now take it slow and easy because you know every step is crucial and must be well calculated. You are willing to let those who are in a hurry pass on by because you know that you can't run at their pace. You can only control your pace and not theirs.

I have a daughter who's a teenager and whenever my wife and I visit someone, she's always ready to go. My words to her are the words of my dad. I tell her that I'm coming slowly but surely. In her mind I'm never coming, but what she doesn't understand is that I'm moving forward. She also doesn't understand the rewards that she would receive by waiting patiently.

Every time my brother and I would go with my father anywhere he would always take us to the store afterwards. He would buy us potato chips, candy, or bubble gum. This would make it all worth the wait. He would buy things for us and say, "I told you that I was coming, slowly but surely." It was his way of rewarding us for hanging in there with his pace. It is my prayer that you live life at the Lord's pace and allow him to reward you because he's coming, slowly but surely! He is looking for those who will never walk back.

"Nothing can stop the man with the right mental attitude from achieving his goal; nothing on earth can help the man with the wrong mental attitude."
Thomas Jefferson (3rd President)

"A brave man is a man who dares to look the Devil in the face and tell him he is a Devil."
James A. Garfield (20th President)

"There are many ways of going forward, but only one way of standing still."
Franklin D. Roosevelt (32nd President)

YOU'RE TOO BLESSED TO BE OFFENDED

It is important to note that new information and new ideas being given to us can easily be pushed aside by those who are easily offended. You must realize that this is not the time to miss out because you are wearing your feelings on your shoulders. Many times because we become so used to doing things the same old way; we are offended by change or an upgrade of any kind. However, we must remember that we are blessed and blessed people move from one level to another.

Many times people hold back the information or wisdom that you need because they feel that you can't handle the truth. You must understand that there is always a better way to do a thing and others have the answer that you've been searching for. You are fortunate to meet people who are honest enough to show you a new and improved way of getting the job done. Don't be insecure or feel that they are trying to put you down.

Jesus told a particular woman that it was not meet to take the children's bread and cast it to dogs. The woman didn't get offended. She wanted the devil to come out of her daughter. Her response was, "Yes, Lord: yet the dogs under the table eat the children's crumbs." Notice this woman kept a positive and respectful attitude towards Jesus. She still called him "Lord." Even though he called her a dog, she still remained focused on what she came to him for instead of being offended.

I am so grateful that I didn't get offended and miss out on my blessing. Brother Kenwin would have never been able to be a blessing to my life if I would have gotten offended. Today this man of God is a pillar in the kingdom of God. He loves his lovely wife, Tasha, and gives the Lord glory and honor in all that he does. As my armor bearer, he constantly does things to keep me strong and healthy. I don't have to beg or pull on him to do anything. He volunteers his help or assistance with a willing heart. He truly loves God and believes in seeking God's face.

As you examine the upgrade that God is striving to make in your life, it is my prayer that you desire it enough not to be offended. God wants to bring you to another place of sharpness. Let him do it as you walk through the pages of this book.

SPIRITUAL UPGRADE

As this year begins we are well aware of the need to upgrade many things around us. People are upgrading their cell phones. They are upgrading their computers. They are upgrading their GPS navigation systems in their cars and they have to upgrade their television sets if they are not digital ready. Yet, I believe with all my heart the greatest upgrade we can make is not natural, but its spiritual. We as believers shouldn't have an up to date computer and a prehistoric walk with God.

I remember years ago being out to lunch with a good friend of mine Pastor Kenneth Anderson. We were in a particular restaurant in Rocky Mount having a wonderful lunch when an older gentleman came over to our table. He was a nice man of God, but he had old and outdated ideas about the God we serve. I stated to him that God was bigger than his dinosaur attitude and unless he changed many of his views about God that the move of God would pass him by or run right over him. His eyes grew big as he looked astonished by my statement. I began to tell him that if he didn't continue to move with God that he wouldn't be around much longer because there wouldn't be a need for him to be here standing in the way of the fresh thing God was doing. In other words, I was challenging him to upgrade himself spiritually so he could remain useful. The Lord was using me to exhort him not to become obsolete. It was a strong anointed exhortation. We must remember that God will not allow anything or anybody to stand in the way of what he desires to do in the lives of his people.

Many weeks went by before I saw this older man of God again, but I eventually did. However, this time he came up to me and told me, "Thank you," for what I said to him and how much he was helped by what I said. He had denounced some of that prehistoric ideology and crossed over into a kingdom of God mentality. He had previously believed that only his denomination was going to heaven, but now he was willing to truly accept his other brothers and sisters in Christ. Today this older man is stronger and healthier than ever. He has upgraded himself, and I truly thank God that he did.

We as the body of Christ must upgrade ourselves spiritually or we will be of no use to bring deliverance to this nation. The word **upgrade** means *"an upward slope or incline, a rising or improving."* In order for God to upgrade us spiritually we must know what our God will use to do it. God will use two basic things to upgrade us. Let's examine them and receive this upgrade.

WHAT DOES GOD USE TO UPGRADE US SPIRITUALLY?

1. God uses His Word
2. God uses a Living Example

God uses his word to make sure our lives improve or rise to another level. Listen at these potent words written by the Apostle Paul,

> II Corinthians 3:18 *"But we all, with open face beholding as in a glass the glory of the Lord, are changed into the same image from glory to glory, even as by the Spirit of the Lord."*

The Amplified says, *"And all of us, as with unveiled face, [because we] continued to behold [in the Word of God] as in a mirror the glory of the Lord, are constantly being transfigured into His very own image in ever increasing splendor and from one degree of glory to another; [for this come] from the Lord [Who is] the Spirit."*

The entrance of God's word into the human spirit brings enlightment and illumination. It causes our lives to increase in splendor as we hearken unto it and strive to live it day by day. When preached or taught properly, it will dethrone warped philosophies given to us from a corrupt or deranged culture.

II Corinthians 10:3-6 *"For though we walk in the flesh, we do not war after the flesh: (For the weapon of our warfare are not carnal, but mighty through God to the pulling down of strong holds;) Casting down imaginations, and every high thing that exalteth itself against the knowledge of God, and bringing into captivity every thought to the obedience of Christ; And having in a readiness to revenge all disobedience when your obedience is fulfilled."*

The Message Translation says, *"The world is unprincipled. It's dog-eat-dog out there! The world doesn't fight fair. But we don't live or fight our battles that way--never have and never will. The tools of our trade aren't for marketing or manipulation, but they are for demolishing that entire massively corrupt culture. We use our powerful God-tools for smashing warped philosophies, tearing down barriers erected against the truth of God, fitting every loose thought and emotion and impulse into the structure of life shaped by Christ. Our tools are ready at hand for clearing the ground of every obstruction and building lives of obedience into maturity."*

The word of God is the only thing that can totally annihilate every ploy the devil has sent to sabotage our lives. The word of God's power can't be denied. It will explode out of your man or woman of God's mouth and clear the path for your victory!

The next thing I wish to elaborate on is that God will use a <u>living example</u> to help upgrade your life. He wants you to learn or glean something by watching others who are good at what they do. He wants you to watch them the way children watch and imitate their parents.

Ephesians 5:1 *"Be ye therefore followers of God, as dear children"*

The Amplified says, *"Therefore Be imitators of God [copy Him and follow His example], as well-beloved children [imitate their father]."*

The Message Bible says, *"Watch what God does, and then do it, like children who learn proper behavior from their parents."*

Our natural mothers and fathers should be unto us an example of what God is like. Unfortunately, this is not the case in many of the homes in our society. Parents haven't embraced the total importance of their role in the lives of their children. Our kids should learn proper behavior from their parents, rather than the streets.

Most people fail to comprehend how important Zacharias and Elisabeth were to the life of John the Baptist. These were godly parents who were given the responsibility of raising the forerunner of Jesus Christ. I believe they took this task very seriously and did a wonderful job in preparing John for his destiny.

We also have to give credit to Joseph and Mary who were chosen to raise Jesus, the Messiah. They had to make sure that Jesus was protected from Herod. They had to know when to return to Egypt with the child. They had to be a couple who feared God and wanted to please him. They were a couple that demonstrated strong faith in God.

There are many couples and single parents who operate like this today. They truly love their children and strive each and every day to raise them up to be godly men and women. However, some of the kids today aren't experiencing this type of discipline and instruction at all. But God can still use pastors, community leaders, teachers, doctors, family members and other believers around you to serve as an example to you. They will help bring about this upgrade God wants you to have.

Hebrew 13:7 *"Remember them which have the rule over you, who have spoken unto you the word of God: whose faith follow, considering the end of their conversation."*

The Amplified says, *"Remember your leaders and superiors in authority [for it was they] who brought to you the Word of God. Observe attentively and consider their manner of living (their outcome of their well spent lives) and imitate their faith (their conviction that God exists and is the Creator and Ruler of all things, the Provider and Bestower of eternal salvation through Christ, and their leaning of the entire human personality on God in absolute trust and confidence in His power, wisdom, and goodness)."*

It is imperative that we have these living examples before us. I appreciate the ones who before they went to be with the Lord served as godly examples to us. Still, God hasn't stop raising up living epistles. He is always trying to get your attention through present day leaders. These leaders will have such an impact on you that eventually your life will sound out as an example to others. As you have followed their lives, others will follow yours.

II Thessalonians 3:7,9 *"For yourselves know how ye ought to follow us: for we behaved not ourselves disorderly among you; Not because we have not power, but to make ourselves an example unto you to follow us."*

I Thessalonians 1:6,7 *"And ye became followers of us, and of the Lord, having received the word in much affliction, with joy of the Holy Ghost: So that ye were examples to all that believe in Macedonia and Achaia."*

The Amplified says, *"And you [set yourselves to] become imitators of us and [through us] of the Lord Himself, for you welcomed our message in [spite of] much persecution, with joy [inspired] by the Holy Spirit; So that you [thus] became a pattern to all the believers(those who adhere to, trust in, and rely on Christ Jesus) in Macedonia and Achaia (most of Greece)."*

Paul was indeed an example unto the Thessalonians. He was willing to make sacrifices in order to give them a pattern to follow. Paul, as well as many men and women of our day, demonstrated several character traits we should look for in the type of examples that will help upgrade our lives.

CHARACTER TRAITS OF A LIVING EXAMPLE

1. Faith and Love

There is no excuse that can be given for us who are naming the name of Christ to not walk by faith and in the love of God. People need to see living individuals demonstrating compassion and concern for others. They need to be impressed by how much we care about the well-being of those around us. Those who we come into contact with must know we love them. Both faith and love require actions being taken by us who say we have the love of God in us. We can't afford to shut up our bowels of compassion.

2. Knowledge & Understanding

We must look to be fed with divine knowledge and understanding from those who are full of knowledge and understanding. We can't upgrade our lives when we are ignorant.

Jeremiah 3:15 *"And I will give you pastors according to mine heart, which shall feed you with knowledge and understanding."*

The Message Bible says, *"I'll give you good shepherd-rulers who rule my way, who rule you with intelligence and wisdom."*

3. Soberness

The living example you need must live a sober life. He or she must be calm, full of self-control and sensible. You can't afford to hang out with those who are full of foolish jesting. You must value those who have serious answers to your serious dilemmas.

4. Righteous Indignation

There will be certain things that the devil will throw at your life that will cause a holy anger to erupt. You need to see people get angry and sin not. These types of examples walk in righteousness and desire to see you walk upright.

5. Live Life In The Spirit

John, the apostle, lived life in the spirit on the isle of Patmos. There are men and women who are mature enough in the spirit who refuse to allow the natural things of life dictate their joy and peace level. These type of people challenge you to upgrade or make significant improvements in your life.

6. Obedience

It is so impressive to rub shoulders with men and women of God who have a burning desire to obey God. These men and women are by no means perfect, but you can't help but notice they are striving to follow God's word and voice as close as possible.

These are the six character traits that you must remain aware of as you look for examples to cause your spiritual life to be raised. We know to be carnally minded is death, but to be spiritual minded is life and peace. I've seen far too many believers in the body of Christ seek to upgrade their natural lives, but lack the desire to upgrade their spiritual life. They upgrade their cell phones, but won't upgrade their thirst in the spirit. Instead, they can only talk about the relationship they used to have with the Lord and not their current one. The devil is not afraid of men and women who have natural upgrades, but no spiritual upgrades. We should have both.

Many of the problems of our day can't be solved with natural inventions alone. These natural upgrades without spiritual upgrades will not get the job done. We must be fully persuaded in our hearts and minds that we need a spiritual upgrade. The Lord is not coming back to check out our natural wit. He will not be impressed by our improvements to make things more comfortable for others if we omit the spiritual side of man.

II Corinthians 5:11 *"Knowing the terror of the Lord, we persuade men, but we are made manifest unto*

Spiritual Upgrade

God: and I trust also are made manifest in your consciences."

The Apostle Paul's states in this verse that he knew the terror of the Lord. The word **terror** used in this verse is the Greek word "phobos" which means <u>fear</u>. The reverence and respect that Paul had for God caused him to speak with vigor. It caused him to overlook people's titles and natural accomplishments and warn them of the judgment to come. He wanted them to be ready spiritually. He preached it with such conviction that it caused Felix to tremble.

Acts 24:25 *"And as he reasoned of righteousness, temperance, and judgment to come, Felix trembled..."*

We must shake this generation into knowing that God wants them to upgrade their spiritual lives before it's too late. This is why we must love and appreciate those who are striving to have the character traits that will help us upgrade or shift our spiritual lives to a whole new level.

UPGRADING OUR PRAYER LIFE

Actors and musicians challenge stores and consumers to buy their upgraded clothing line, yet we need the clergy to challenge God's people to upgrade their prayer life. It would be a vital mistake to upgrade our clothes and allow the adversary to defeat us because we don't pray. The disciples of Jesus saw him praying and asked him to teach them how to pray.

> Luke 11:1 *"And it came to pass, that, as he was praying in a certain place, when he ceased, one of his disciples said unto him, Lord, teach us to pray, as John also taught his disciples."*

We can never say we are rising or improving spiritually without upgrading our prayer life. Our heavenly Father is challenging us to call unto him. He knows what he can do for those who will upgrade themselves in prayer.

Psalms 91:15 "He shall call upon me, and I will answer him: I will be with him in trouble; I will deliver him, and honour him."

The Message Bible says, *"Call me and I'll answer, be at your side in bad times; I'll rescue you, then throw you a party."*

You and I both know that these are indeed perilous times in which we are living in. Many people are experiencing trouble due to floods, hurricanes, earthquakes, gang violence, terrorism, and etc. We must believe that it's time to call upon our God like we have never called on him before. God said he would give you a party. I don't believe anyone can throw a party for you like God can. He will bring out the best of everything. He has promised to rescue you and shower you with a pull out all the stops party!

Jeremiah 33:3 "Call unto me, and I will answer thee, and show thee great and mighty things, which thou knowest not."

As we examine upgrading your prayer life, I will strive to unfold some of the revelatory things that God has revealed to me about prayer that I know and hope will be helpful to you. I will begin by telling you that **prayer demands a reverence for God and faith in God.** Those who do not fear or respect God will not pray, neither will those who lack faith in God.

> Psalms 10:4 *"The wicked, through the pride of his countenance, will not seek after God: God is not in all his thoughts."*

> Acts 10:1,2 *"There was a certain man in Caesarea called Cornelius, a centurion of the Italian band, A devout man, and one that feared God with all his house, which gave much alms to the people, and prayed to God always."*

These two verses show us the tremendous contrast between the wicked and the righteous. The wicked don't seek after God, but the righteous do. We have a respect for who God is and what he can do when we cry out to him in faith. This is why we can't rely on how we prayed ten or twenty years ago. We must know that God wants us to call upon him today as we face today's trials and tests. He knows he has your answer, and he will answer you when you pray.

Our fellowship with God through prayer is important to our confidence in him. This is what made Jesus so confident in his Father. He was intimate with the Father through prayer. He knew the Father that he fellowshipped with each day wouldn't fail him. His faith in prayer was tremendous and Jesus kept it up to date. He didn't allow ministry or attending to the needs of others to become more important than praying to the Father.

We have to be very careful not to allow our education and natural intelligence to remove our faith in prayer. Our fellowship with brilliant people of our day still can't produce for us what fellowshipping with God can produce for us. Because some men can achieve some things without reliance on God they allow prayer to be an after thought. Jesus never did that. He dwelt among great minds, but he knew great thoughts are vain unless they align with the thoughts of the Father. He knew through fellowship with God what to ask and what not to ask. His prayer appointments were never missed. He showed up for them all. The same way we go to the doctor or dentist because we have appointments to keep with them is the same way we must make and keep our prayer appointments with God. This is why Jesus didn't waiver about any request he made to the Father.

Our faith in prayer has to be unshakeable. We must believe that great things will show up in response to our cry. In order to boldly go where no man has gone before we have to exemplify faith in our prayers. Nothing can change people and things like prayer!

EIGHT THINGS TO KNOW ABOUT PRAYER

1. Prayer is private and personal

It is not a show off type of thing or something you do to impress people. It is be done in secret to receive open rewards from God.

Mark 1:35 *"And in the morning, rising up a great while before day, he went out, and departed into a solitary place, and there prayed."*

Luke 5:16 *"And he with withdrew himself into the wilderness, and prayed."*

The Message Bible says, *"As often as possible Jesus withdrew to out-of-the-way places for prayer."*

Matthew 6:6 *"But thou, when thou prayest, enter into thy closet, and when thou hast shut thy door, pray to thy Father which is in secret; and thy Father which seeth in secret shall reward thee openly."*

2. **Prayer is monologue**

There are times when we are talking to God and not waiting for a response from him. For example, when you pray over your food or give thanks to God for it, you don't wait twenty or thirty minutes to hear God speak back. You just simply give him a prayer of thanksgiving and eat your meal.

St. Matthew 15:36 "And he took the seven loaves and the fishes, and gave thanks..."

3. **Prayer is dialogue**

We must be aware of the fact that we serve a God who not only will listen to us, but we serve a God who will talk back. He will speak to our hearts and minds with an exact answer in accordance to the petition we make to him. David, who asked God should he pursue the Philistines or not, heard God talk directly back to him. Paul, who asked the Lord who he was, heard the Lord reply, "I am Jesus of Nazareth..." It is two way communication.

Philippians 4:6 "Be careful for nothing; but in everything by prayer and supplication with thanksgiving let your request be made known unto God."

4. Prayer is corporate and inclusive

Acts 12:5 *"Peter therefore was kept in prison: but prayer was made without ceasing of the church unto God for him."*

This particular verse plainly reveals to us the power and the deliverance that comes as a result of corporate prayer. When the church comes together as a united front, we can see change through our prayers.

5. Prayer is to be done with understanding or your own language

I Corinthians 14:15 *"What is it then? I will pray with the spirit, and I will pray with understanding also; I will sing with the spirit, and I will sing with the understanding also."*

6. Prayer is to be done in an unknown tongue or language

I Corinthians 14:14 *"For if I pray in an unknown tongue, my spirit prayeth, but my understanding is unfruitful."*

I wish to take a few moments and elaborate on this type of praying because I can truly say this is one of the most effective ways of praying. You are never inaccurate when you are alone praying in the spirit. You are speaking mysteries in the spirit unto God.

Spiritual Upgrade

You are always praying in line with the perfect will of God when you pray this way. Your spirit is talking to God and many potent things are being uttered. This type of praying opens up the spiritual realm to you and I in a whole new way that praying in our natural language can never do. There are many things that I've discovered about my destiny and purpose through praying in an unknown tongue. There are also many things I've been able to endure because I was able to pray in an unknown tongue. This type of prayer is so neglected and I believe many believers are not as strong inwardly as they could be because of failing to pray this way.

As you continue to pray this way, the Heavenly Father will begin to give you the interpretations of many of the things you are praying about. All you have to do is ask him and believe him for the interpretation, and he will begin to unfold to your heart and mind some of these prophetic things being prayed in the Holy Ghost. This is supernatural and worth every moment of your prayer time. The Apostle Paul prayed this way often when he was alone. In the church or local assembly, he prayed in a way they could understand him. But when he was in private, Paul prayed in an unknown tongue more than anyone in the church because no one in the church had to endure the kind of opposition and persecution that he had to endure.

I Corinthians 14:18 *"I thank my God, I speak in tongues more than you all"*

This is why I believe your pastor, bishop, or overseer should pray this way more than anyone in the church. This will not be done in a public way to be seen of the members, so they can think you are so spiritual. It will be done because we as men and women of God out front are always under some kind of attack. We have to keep our spiritual strength in line to be able to keep so many people encouraged. Your natural language which comes from your mind or intellect is not sufficient when you're experiencing serious warfare or attacks. You will run out of words, and you will not be able to find sufficient words to utter. It is at this time the Holy Spirit will utter words through your spirit that will be more than appropriate to bring you through with power and might. He knows how to pray in line with God's perfect will.

7. **Prayer can be short and to the point**

We don't have to nor should we try to pray long prayers just to say we prayed a long time. Prayers are not answered in accordance to their length. Because some people try to pray long prayers, they start repeating the same words they have already said. This doesn't have to be done when you pray. When you are finish praying, don't try to impress men by going on with a long prayer. God will answer those who pray short and to the point.

Some people don't enjoy the power and victory of their prayer life because they are trying to pray a long prayer like somebody else they heard pray.

8. Prayer can be long and searching for the point

Luke 6:12 *"And it came to pass in those days, that he went out into a mountain to pray, and continued all night in prayer to God."*

You and I need to know these eight things in order to begin to bring an upgrade to our prayer life. But let's take it a few steps further. Once these things are known, I need to know what it takes to get prayer to work.

FIVE THINGS WE MUST BE IN PRAYER

There are five basic things we must be in order to get results in prayer or to make prayer work. As we look at them, I know you will be enlightened.

1. **Earnest**

The word **earnest** means "to put one's whole self into something." I believe many times we don't pray heart-felt prayers. This hinders the response that we get and causes us to waiver in our faith. We need to pray about things that really will moves our hearts. This is why the book of James teaches us the one who is afflicted needs to pray because he feels it and will throw his whole self into his prayers.

> James 5:13 *"Is any among you afflicted? let him pray. Is any merry? let him sing psalms."*

Luke 22:44 *"And being in an agony he prayed more earnestly: and his sweat was as to were great drops of blood falling down to the ground."*

James 5:16 *"....The effectual fervent prayer of a righteous man availed much."*

The Amplified says, *"....The earnest (heartfelt, continued) prayer of a righteous man makes tremendous power available [dynamic in its working]."*

2. Unwearied

We must not faint or get tired in prayer. We must be like the widow who refused to grow weary in her pursuit of the unjust judge. Jesus doesn't want us to grow weary in prayer.

Luke 18:1 *"And he spake a parable unto them to this end, that men ought always to pray, and not to faint."*

The Message Bible says, *"Jesus told them a story that it was necessary for them to pray consistently and never quit."*

The Amplified says, *"Also [Jesus] told them a parable to the effect that they ought always to pray and not to turn coward (faint, lose heart, and give up)."*

3. Steadfast In Prayer

Colossians 4:2 *"Continue in prayer, and watch in the same with thanksgiving"*

The Amplified says, *"Be earnest and unwearied and steadfast in your prayer [life], being [both] alert and intent in [your praying] with thanksgiving."*

4. Alert

The word <u>alert</u> means "to be watchful and wide-awake." It means "to be ready at any instant for what is coming." The day in which we live calls for us to be saints who will live our lives this way. We should totally understand the importance of our prayer life to the people we fellowship with and the nations around us. Even though God may not tell us everything that is about to happen; his word gives us enough to prepare for what is ahead. Prayer keeps our spirit or inner man prepared for the unexpected. It keeps us strong inwardly so that the trouble or crisis of our times don't move us. Through prayer we are postured to be ready for anything we face in this life with renewed courage and vigor.

5. Intent

We, who are the called of God, must not grow disinterested in prayer and the Father's will. Our desire to see God's will done in our lives and others should drive us to our knees. We must fix our thoughts earnestly on seeing the purposes of God being fulfilled. We must pay attention to what we are asking the Heavenly Father and not just utter words. Once we have searched out the holy scriptures and allowed God's word to dominate our minds, then we must pray with a direct result in mind. We must fix our eyes on that request and believe it will come to pass.

We must also be aware of the main reason we pray, which is to receive the grace we need. As we upgrade our prayer life, we are also upgrading the grace of God in our life. It is his grace that keeps us strong and causes us not to yield to the temptations that we face. His grace keeps us from falling apart. This is why we must keep our prayer life up to date.

Hebrews 4:16 *"Let us therefore come boldly unto the throne of grace, that we may obtain mercy, and find grace to help in time of need."*

UPGRADING OUR COMMITMENT

Proverbs 16:3 *"Commit thy works unto the Lord, and thy thought shall be established."*

The Amplified says, *"Roll your works upon the Lord [commit and trust them wholly to Him: He will cause your thoughts to become agreeable to His will, and] so shall your plans be established and succeed."*

New International Version says, *"Commit to the LORD whatever you do, and your plans will succeed."*

The Message Bible says, *"Put God in charge of your work, then what you've planned will take place."*

I believe it would be a waste of time to write a book talking about spiritual upgrade without speaking about commitment. Many of us know people who are committed to natural things but demonstrate little or no commitment to God and his kingdom. This is an absolute tragedy and must not continue to exist in the body of Christ. If we are going to be committed to anyone it should be God. He is always there when we need him and has given us so much. All of us should be willing to upgrade our commitment to him the same way people are upgrading our television sets.

Many people fail to upgrade their commitment to God because they think they can control God. However, those of us who are born again recognize nothing can be further from the truth. God is in charge. He is the maker of man. It is God who made us and not we ourselves. In fact, notice this powerful verse written by Paul to the saints in Corinth,

I Corinthians 10:14 *"Wherefore, my dearly beloved, flee from idolatry."*

The Message Bible says, *"So my dear friends, when you see people reducing God to something they can use or control, get out of their company as fast as you can."*

According to these verses, we shouldn't love or venerate anything more than God. We shouldn't strive to make God small and make man big. The desire of our soul should be to exalt God or allow our soul to make a boast in the Lord. You and I were created to glorify the Lord. We must get away from those who don't have an attitude of gratitude. We can't afford to continue to associate with those who are striving to be their own master. Neither can we continue to walk with those who act like God doesn't know what he is doing. We must remember God is working all things according to the counsel of his will.

Ephesians 1:11 *"In whom also we have obtained an inheritance, being predestinated according to the purpose of him who worketh all things after the counsel of his own will."*

God's will reveals to us that he wants us to have the best in life. It shows us his wisdom and prudence towards his people. You and I must demonstrate a commitment to seeing his will done in our lives. Therefore, our thoughts have to be thoughts according to his good pleasure. God would have never allowed Jesus to suffer like he did, unless he wanted us to experience the riches of his grace. We must be fully persuaded that God is bringing to pass his will in our lives even when it doesn't look like it or feel like it. This is why it is so important that we hang with those who have a revelation of this.

Those who understand the will of God being done in your life will encourage you to maintain your commitment. They will say things that will cause you to be more determined to walk in line with his will. They know God is moving you out of the old and into the new. They won't allow you to cast away your confidence in your God.

Spiritual Upgrade

Hebrews 10:35,36 *"Cast not away therefore your confidence, which hath great recompence of reward. For ye have need of patience, that, after ye have done the will of God, ye might receive the promise."*

The Message Bible says,. *"So don't throw it all away now. You were sure of yourselves then. It's still a sure thing! But you need to stick it out, staying with God's plan so you'll be there for the promised completion"*

Those who don't understand the will of God will speak foolish things that will try to cause you to stop being committed. Don't listen to them. You have a reward to get from God and you're too close to relinquish your commitment. I agree with the Message Bible which says, "It's a sure thing!" Only a fool will give up on a sure thing. I'm no fool and neither are you. This means we will hold fast to our confidence and rejoicing firm to the end. This is what Moses and Jesus Christ did. Moses was faithful as a servant appointed by God, but Christ was faithful as the owner of the house.

Hebrews 3:5,6 *"And Moses verily was faithful in all his house, as a servant, for a testimony of those things which were to be spoken after; But Christ as a son over his own house; whose house are we, if we hold fast the confidence and the rejoicing of the hope firm unto the end."*

Christ as the owner of everything was highly committed. He was faithful as the man in charge. This verse tells us that the only way that we prove that we are the house of Christ is by holding on to our commitment. Those of us who truly believe are still rejoicing now like we did when we first believed. Our faith hasn't wavered. We believe it today the same way we did when God first told us. We know that he can bring to pass his own words. We rejoice in the hope of everything turning out just like God promised. He's able to keep his word. We are committed to the end.

The people we associate with must know what it takes to upgrade our commitment to God and his kingdom. You and I must upgrade our commitment and encourage others to upgrade their commitment as well. This will require us to be faithful to God and his work at a whole new level. One of the scriptures I believe the Holy Spirit really needs the body of Christ to believe and act on is written in the Old Testament by one of the wisest men who ever walked the earth.

> Proverbs 28:20 *"A faithful man shall abound in blessings: but he that maketh haste to be rich shall not be innocent."*

So many dynamic things await you and I when we have been faithful to God's heavenly agenda. He is always looking for faithful people. Everybody will say they've been faithful, but the truth of the matter is that faithful men and women are rare. They are not easily found even though they are constantly being sought.

> Proverbs 20:6 *"Most men will proclaim every one his own goodness: but a faithful man who can find?"*

The type of commitment that is being sought is undaunted when things get rough. It doesn't waiver because things are not going the way you have planned. It is the type of faithfulness and commitment that can't be intimidated or made to back down. This type of commitment and faithfulness has its conscience ruled by the word of God. It is the type of commitment that you will only find in a few good men and women. It will not be found in the titles, but true leaders indeed.

> "A leader, once convinced a particular course of action is the right one, must have the determination to stick with it and be undaunted when the going gets rough."
> **Ronald Reagan** (40th President)

This is not the time to be slack in our commitment. It is time to tighten our grip and plant our feet on the rock of God's word. God expects us to commit this work to faithful men. They will be able to teach others and never quit.

> II Timothy 2:1,2 *"Thou Therefore, my son, be strong in the grace that is in Christ Jesus. And the*

things that thou hast heard of me among many witnesses, the same commit thou to faithful men, who shall be able to teach others also."

The great leaders of our day can't afford to not challenge God's people to a new level of commitment and faithfulness. It is a requirement of our day. Nothing great will ever happen through the slothful and uncommitted. We must take our stand and refuse to promote the unfaithful. No matter how gifted and talented people are we must keep our eyes on the faithful in the land. Never let the unfaithful intimidate you.

"I cannot be intimidated from doing that which my judgment and conscience tell me is right by any earthly power."
Andrew Jackson (7th President)

We must continue to remind ourselves that God is faithful and he preserves the faithful. As long as you and I keep our commitment level upgraded and don't allow it to slip, we will be taken care of by God Almighty, and there is nothing the devil can do about it.

Psalm 31:23 *"O love the Lord, all ye his saints: for the Lord preserveth the faithful, and plentifully rewardeth the proud doer."*

THREE THINGS WE MUST BE IN ORDER TO UPGRADE OUR COMMITMENT

1. We must be **informed**

> Proverbs 20:18 *"Every purpose is established by counsel: and with good advice make war."*

> The Message Bible says, *"Form your purpose by asking for counsel, then carry it out using all the help you can get."*

We must surround ourselves with people who aren't throwing out information that hasn't been tried or proven. We must gather together all the facts from those who have a proven track record and information that will help us upgrade ourselves in the kingdom of God.

2. We must be **inspired**

Romans 12:11 *"Not slothful in business; fervent in spirit; serving the Lord"*

The Amplified says, *"Never lag in zeal and in earnest endeavor; be aglow and burning with the Spirit, serving the Lord."*

The Message Bible says, *"Don't burn out, keep yourselves fueled and aflame."*

3. We must be **involved**

I hope you noticed that I intentionally placed being informed before inspired because too many people make decisions or moves in life based on inspiration. They don't fully count up the cost. I believe when this happens the commitment will be short-lived. We need believers who are committed for the long haul. We want to see you go all the way. This is why you need to be inspired by information and not just what sounds like a good idea.

It is also important to know that your commitment will attract Satanic attacks. The devil hears you testify that you are going all the way with your spiritual commitment. He will plot to get you to retract your statement or confession. You must really be determined to upgrade yourself or you will be cheated out of the good things your commitment will attract.

THREE THINGS YOUR COMMITMENT WILL ATTRACT

1. *Your commitment will attract **POWER***

The power of God will never be attracted to those who will not forsake all to be a servant of the Most High. Your commitment to your local church and the body of Christ is very important. You can't be an unfaithful servant and walk in the power of God. As a young nineteen year old Christian, I remember being totally mesmerized by the power of God. I not only read about it in the Bible, but watched it demonstrated through my pastor, Apostle Marvin Smith. This man flowed in the awesome power of God. His Pastor, Apostle John Barber, also walked in the power of God. I saw the power of God up close. It was absolutely life changing. These men of God and many others of our day like Shambach and Rod Parsley have a high level of commitment.

Spiritual Upgrade

I can recall a particular service in the city of Goldsboro N.C. I was a young minister at this time and still being groomed. I saw my pastor and his pastor point directly at individuals and call out their conditions, lay hands on them, and the power of God heal them. This was common place in our church and the places I would travel with my pastor.

This particular night, Apostle John Barber was preaching in Goldsboro at a particular church. The building was packed with standing room only. After he ministered the word, the Lord began to use him in the gifts of the Spirit. I saw him call out a particular young man and minister many wholesome things to him. Then Apostle Baber said that he saw the initials over the young man's head "DD." The gentleman fell under the power of God. I was anxious to ask the young man what his name was after the service. Once the service came to an end, I rushed out of the sanctuary passing everyone in my path, determined to get an opportunity to speak to this young man. When I finally got to him and asked him what was his name, guess what he said? He said his name was Danny Davis.

These types of expressions of God's power can only be achieved by those with high levels of commitment. We can't expect to see the power of God with little or no commitment. You can't show up when you want to or do things on your own time in the kingdom of God. We would be fired from our natural jobs if we approached them with this type of attitude. If man's level of commitment is high for his corporation, then surely God's expectation of our commitment to him and his kingdom must be high as well. The power of God will follow your commitment.

2. Your commitment will attract **WEALTH**

The raise or wealth you desire is predicated on your commitment to God. We are admonished over and over in scripture to know that our rewards come from the Lord. Those who are in the body of Christ who have any kind of wealth, demonstrate high levels of commitment. They are committed to serve God no matter what. They are committed to tithe no matter what. They are committed to their families no matter what. They walk in wealth and people persecute them. But people never want to give them credit for their commitment to hard work. Yet those of us who have anything in life as it relates to the financial arena know that we've had to be committed while we saw others give up and walk away. It has now led us to the wealth that was prepared for us by the Lord.

Psalms 128:1,2 *"Blessed is every one that feareth the Lord; that walketh in his ways. For thou shalt eat the labour of thine hands: happy shalt thou be, and it shall be well with thee."*

The New International Version says, *"Blessed are all who fear the Lord, who walk in his ways. You will eat the fruit of your labour; blessings and prosperity will be yours."*

The Message Bible says, *"All you who fear God, how blessed you are! how happily you walk his*

Spiritual Upgrade

---

smooth straight road! You worked hard and deserve all you've got coming. Enjoy the blessing! Revel in the goodness!

3. *Your commitment will attract* **FAVOR or THE HELP OF OTHERS**

Many times people see favor in your life and try to attribute it to something other than your commitment to complete the task. God will send the right people across your path if you put forth a sincere commitment. He knows the assignment is too big for one person to achieve.

Psalm 5:12 *"For thou, Lord, wilt bless the righteous; with favour wilt thou compass him as with a shield."*

Exodus 3:21 *"And I will give this this people favour in the sight of the Egyptians: and it shall come to pass, that, when ye go, ye shall not go empty."*

WHY AREN'T PEOPLE COMMITTED TO GOD AND HIS KINGDOM?

Seeing these types of blessings and benefits awaits the committed, you are probably wondering like I am why aren't people committed? Why won't they upgrade their commitment and go after these things the Father wants them to enjoy? Let's examine some of the reasons why.

1. <u>They won't repent</u>

Refusing to repent is one of the first reasons people aren't committed as they ought to be to God and his kingdom. It is important to know that the God who created you will always give you space to repent. His mercy endureth forever. You have to be willing to upgrade your life and if that means admitting you have done something wrong, so be it. Repentance is your way of getting your commitment upgraded.

Spiritual Upgrade

---

2. <u>They won't organize</u>

The word **organize** means "to put into working order." It is very hard to be committed to anything if you don't get organized. You have to put first things first. Sometimes one of the hardest things in the world to get people to do is to get organized. They tend to get use to disorder and chaos. Sometimes women tend to be better at organizing than men. However, I've seen men who are highly developed in this area and are experiencing a dynamic life of commitment in the kingdom.

My wife is one of the most organized people I know. She does nothing without a receipt or putting it in her PDA. She also has a pda/smart phone and many other technological gadgets to help her stay organized. Anything that helps her keep things organized, I allow her to purchase it, because I know this helps us keep up with our obligations. If you are a very busy person which I know you probably are, you must make sure you stay organized.

3. <u>They won't forgive</u>

Living a life free of offense has to be the goal of every committed individual. People will do or say things to hurt your feelings. But remember they are not your source, God is. You must choose to forgive or release them. You must recognize that you made a commitment to God and not to man. You must keep your vow to God, your pastor, and your local church. The Lord has been too good to you and I for us to allow anyone to destroy our commitment to him. Forgive and move on.

4. They are afraid

We must be aware of the fact that we can't be committed if we are afraid. We must not allow bad experiences of the past to keep us from being committed to God and his kingdom. You must allow your love for God and people to cause you to cast this fear aside. The rewards are too great and the devil will tell you all kinds of lies to keep you in fear so you will not commit yourself to the work of God. Everybody is not a crook or out to use and hurt you. God will guard and protect you if you trust him.

Psalm 56:3,4 *"What time I am afraid, I will trust in thee. In God I will praise his word, in God I have put my trust; I will not fear what flesh can do unto me."*

Psalm 55:22,23 *"Cast thy burden upon the Lord, and he shall sustain thee; he shall never suffer the righteous to be moved. But thou, O God, shalt bring them down into the pit of destruction: bloody and deceitful men shall not live out half their days; but I will trust in thee.*

The adversary has used fear to hinder people's giving and sacrifice of time. Television shows and some of the news media have used their programs to show the negative side of preachers and the body of Christ. They don't understand that we preach about a perfect man, Jesus Christ, who came to seek and to save that which was lost. He delivered us for our sins and justified us.

> **Romans 4:24,25** *"But for us also, to whom it shall be imputed, if we believe on him that raised up Jesus our Lord from the dead; Who was delivered for our offences, and was raised for our justification."*

You and I don't have to be afraid to have a high level of commitment to Jesus because he's the one that we serve. We are in the kingdom to serve him with our whole heart and since he justified us, it is the least we can do. No matter what fears Satan seeks to bring to your mind, you must show him that they are not good enough. Yes, they may be legitimate fears, but they are not enough to stop me from trusting God or be totally committed to him. You are well aware of the fact that God is big enough to handle anyone who seeks to mishandle you. Go in Faith, not in Fear!

4. They won't be patient

We are not a bunch of naive individuals who believe in a get rich quick scheme. We are well aware of the commitment and sacrifice it is going to take to achieve the level of success we desire. We know we have to continue to be as patient in the kingdom as we were when we served the devil. Many people have given the devil forty and fifty years of their lives. Yet, when they get saved, they want everything to turn around in one year. This is not how it usually works. You have to stay the course before you see significant change in your life. This builds character in you and allows others to see you mean business.

I Corinthians 15:58 *"Therefore, my beloved brethren, be ye steadfast, unmoveable, always abounding in the work of the Lord, forasmuch as ye know that your labour is not in vain in the Lord."*

The Amplified says, *"Therefore, my beloved, be firm (steadfast), immovable, always abounding in the work of the Lord [always being superior, excelling, doing more than enough in the service that your labor in the Lord is not futile [it is never wasted or to no purpose]."*

The Message Bible says, *"With all this going for us, my dear, dear, friends, stand your ground. And don't hold back. Throw yourselves into the work of the Master, confident that nothing you do for him is a waste of time."*

It is important for you to always be aware of the <u>fact</u> that your labor is never a waste of time. You must fully throw yourself into it and watch God bless the work of your hands. You will always receive the promise, if you let patience have it's complete work in you. Stand your ground. Let every devil know that you are aware of what you have going for you. This is what being spiritual is all about. It is not being spooky, instead it is making sure that we are talking and thinking in line with the word of God. We refuse to give up because of what God said he would do in our lives.

Spiritual Upgrade

Many times we let go because we don't acknowledge what we have in our favor. We are too busy focusing in on what is opposing us that we fail to acknowledge the things on our side to help us win. His word gives us the advantage in every area of our lives. It causes us to live life a step ahead of those around us.

UPGRADING OUR OPEN DOOR

I Corinthians 16:9 *"For a great door and effectual is opened unto me, and there are many adversaries."*

The Message says, *"A huge door of opportunity for good works has opened up here. There is also mushrooming opposition."*

One of the most exciting things about being a believer in the Lord Jesus Christ is not knowing what person or persons your life will impact next. In spite of Paul's opposition, he was determined to preach the gospel through the door God had opened up for him. We must remember the church is a called out group, who have been chosen in Christ before the foundation of the world, to bring healing and deliverance to the world. This means that you and I will be given opportunities to share the gospel with people in many different states and countries. We have no idea where or when this will happen; therefore, we must continue to upgrade our open door. We must not get stuck into believing that the God we serve wants us to keep witnessing to the same two people who know you already. God doesn't want you week after week to witness to the same persons who show little or no interest. Instead, he will lead you to an entirely different city. Or in the mall he will call upon you to share your faith with someone who doesn't know you at all and they will accept Christ. This is what keeps our lives exciting and refreshed. God is always opening up these types of opportunities for us because he desires to see men and women set free from the power of the enemy. He wants them to be saved. We must always stay ready and never be ashamed to share our faith with a lost and dying world.

II Corinthians 2:12 *"Furthermore, when I came to Troas to preach Christ's gospel, and a door was opened unto me of the Lord"*

The door that the Lord opens for us must not be taken for granted. It could mean life or death for somebody. I remember years ago while sitting at home with my wife on a Saturday night enjoying each others company and the telephone rang. A woman was on the other end of the phone. I could hear the fear in her voice as I answered her call. She had a young man who was her cousin over to her house trying to witness to him. The young man had a gun in his hand and was about to kill himself. She was trying to

Spiritual Upgrade

stay calm, yet I could tell the fear was there. She said to me, "Pastor Sharpe talk to him please, don't let him kill himself." She told me that the gun was in a cocked (ready to be fired) position. I tried to keep her as calm as I could. She said she didn't know who else to call. The young man had heard about our ministry through another young man who was a member of our church at the time. I whispered to my wife as to what was going on, and she began to pray. Thank God for a saved, praying wife. As I was praying in a silent way and in the Holy Spirit, I asked the lady to allow me to speak to him. I began to minister to him being led by the Lord and he put the gun down. He began to weep on the phone as I shared with him how much the Lord loved him and wanted to make something great out of his life. I asked him to give the gun and the phone to his cousin and told her to bring him to the sanctuary the next day. The young man came that Sunday and gave his life to the Lord. He is still alive today.

I've also been blessed to be able to preach the gospel on several radio stations as well as television stations. These doors of opportunity have given me a chance to help many lives and I expect bigger doors to continue to open. I remember one particular incident that still gives me chills today when I think about it. This was when cassette tapes were very popular. There were no such thing as a cd or dvd. My wife, Resunester went to deliver the cassette to the radio station that particular Saturday morning for me. I had preached out of town on Friday night and in order to allow me to rest for Sunday service, she took the cassette. Her brother, Frankie was living in Wilson, N.C. at that particular time where the station was located. She wanted to spend some time with him at his newly rented apartment. He had taken her to the station, and I had to pick her up. I arrived at the station and asked her if she exchanged the tapes. She said, "Yes," and we drove out of the station's parking lot. As we were about a mile away, it was about time for our broadcast to come on the radio. I was driving, so I asked her to turn the radio to the station because it was about time for our broadcast. But instead of playing the cassette I gave her, she made a mistake and brought back the same cassette I had given her. I was totally shocked and disappointed as I heard our broadcast playing the same program that I had heard the previous Saturday. I couldn't believe it. I asked her how in the world did this happen. She said she had made a mistake while the owner of the station and she were chatting. Somehow the station manager had given her back the same tape. None of this seemed to be a good enough excuse for me. I was still hot about it. I didn't even want to hear the broadcast. I remember telling my wife to turn the radio off because I couldn't bear listening to it. My wife stated that she wanted to listen to it and refused to turn it off. She said to me these potent words that would prove to be prophetic later on, "How do you know whether or not God wanted the same broadcast to be played to help somebody." When she said these words, I began to hear the witness in my spirit and I said to her, "You are right. The Lord might have

Spiritual Upgrade

somebody that he is trying to reach." What happened next was an absolute miracle!

When we arrived back home to our house in Rocky Mount N.C., the telephone rang. A young lady was on the other end and what she expressed to me was absolutely astounding. She had been going through many things in her life and the devil had started to talk to her. She said that she had gotten so depressed that she couldn't take anymore and the devil began to talk to her about killing her children. She had gone into the kitchen and turned her oven on as high as she could get it. She was getting ready to open the oven and put her two little daughters inside and cook them. But before she could put her daughters inside the oven, our radio broadcast came on. This particular broadcast had caused her mind to get back on the right track and she got encouraged and built up by the word of God. She kept saying, "Pastor Sharpe, I thank God for using you and I thank God for your radio broadcast." I asked her did she listen to the broadcast often. She said every Saturday, but she had missed last Saturday. However, she was grateful that she heard it this Saturday.

Isn't this just like God! This particular woman had missed the broadcast and God knew she needed to hear it, so he allowed my wife to take the broadcast that day. He allowed her to get caught up in a conversation that would cause the station manager to give her back the wrong tape. He allowed my wife not to notice it because he wanted to keep this lady from committing a heinous crime. God wanted to keep those two young girls alive. Hallelujah! Hallelujah!

Spiritual Upgrade

This lady was being harassed by the adversary, but God sent his word and delivered her from destruction. This happened on Saturday and she came to visit our local assembly that Sunday morning. She was a very lovely lady and the little girls were about three and four years old. It was absolutely gorgeous. I truly praise God for the door of opportunity he gave me to be on the radio at that time.

I also have been blessed to help many people through the books we've written. The first book we wrote is entitled, "<u>HOW TO OVERPOWER DISCOURAGEMENT</u>." It was out for about two weeks when a powerful testimony was given to me. A young man had purchased it from one of our members. He thought he was buying it for himself, but he had no idea he was really buying it for his father until one day his father was at home in his living room and was about to commit suicide. His father had a gun pointed to his head and was about to blow his brains out. He was weeping and telling his dad not to do it. His dad stated he was tired of trying to go on.

The young man grabbed the book and told his dad to please read the book before he committed suicide. So, his dad with one hand on the gun and the other hand reading the book, he fell on his knees and surrendered his life to Christ. The words from the book set him free. Thank you Jesus!

I wish to share another testimony about the book at this time. I was at Newness of Life Christian Center one Sunday Morning just about to go up into the pulpit and preach when one of the ushers told me

Spiritual Upgrade

the telephone was for me. I knew it had to be important because the ushers wouldn't have bothered me at this time unless it was something pressing. The usher stated to me that it was the Greenville, N.C. Sherriff on the phone. I didn't know what to expect seeing I was being called by the Sherriff on a Sunday morning. I answered the phone and the Sherriff asked me if I was Pastor Van Sharpe? I replied, "Yes, how can I help you?" He said, "I need you to be praying, because we are on the phone with a young man who is about to commit suicide. He has somehow heard you on radio, so if we can get to him in time will it be okay if we bring him to your service?" I told him it would be fine.

As I was about fifteen or twenty minutes from finishing the sermon, I noticed this young man in the audience. Once the message was finished, he asked to speak to me. I told him I was glad to get a chance to meet him and I was glad he came to the service. He began to share why he wanted to kill himself. He desired to take his life because a young lady that he thought truly loved him had decided to end their relationship. He was devastated. I told him that I knew exactly what he was dealing with and I handed him the book entitled, "HOW TO OVERPOWER DISCOURAGEMENT." I told him that I wanted him to promise to read the book and let the Lord have his way in his life.

About two years later, this young man came back to visit us. He gave the testimony about how he read the book and gave his life to God. The Lord had filled him with the Holy Ghost and blessed him with a Holy

Spiritual Upgrade

Ghost filled wife. They were in a good local church and he wanted to tell me how much the book had helped him to get his life on track with God. Bless the Wonderful name of Jesus!

I hope these testimonies are stirring you to know and understand the importance of upgrading your open door. We are living in a glorious day of all kinds of technological breakthroughs. I believe one of the main reasons is so that people can be exposed to the gospel of Jesus Christ. We don't have to allow our ministry to become obsolete, but rather upgrade the ministry and expand the kingdom of God.

I don't believe I would be able to say I've done this book justice unless I also talk about one of the many testimonies we receive through our television outreach. It happened on a day when I was checking on a scholarship for my daughter, who is currently a student at North Carolina A&T University. I went into this building in Tarboro to speak to a particular young man, when I was approached by an elderly white gentleman. This elderly gentleman said that he enjoyed our television broadcast. He said that his daughter's life had been totally changed because of it. He told me that his daughter had gotten so depressed that she had checked into a hotel. She had purchased pills and a gun. She had planned to commit suicide in the hotel. She had her television on and while sitting on the bed with the gun she started flipping through the channels. While flipping through the channels, she paused on the station where I was preaching the gospel. She said to herself, "I know that man. He's my high school classmate. That's Van Sharpe." She kept the television on the station and continued to listen to the word of God. As a result of the power of God and his word, she didn't kill herself. She's alive today and I'm grateful to God for it. Hallelujah, my former classmate is still alive! God is good! These are the type of things that are truly satisfying in life. They give our lives significance.

> Acts 20:24 *"But none of these things move me, neither count I my life dear unto myself, so that I might finish my course with joy, and the ministry, which I have received of the Lord Jesus, to testify the gospel of the grace of God."*

The New Living Translation says, *"My life is worth nothing unless I use it for doing the work assigned me by the Lord Jesus—The work of telling others the Good News about God's wonderful kindness and love."*

How many of us can truly say that this is our attitude about our lives? Unless we are telling people about Jesus our lives are worthless. This doesn't have to be done in the sanctuary. I can also recall leading people to the Lord on the Trail way Bus when I was in college. Today I've led people to the Lord in barbershops, beauty parlors, Food Lions, Wal-Mart, and etc.

We should pray for our pastors, leaders, and members that God would open a door of utterance for them to speak the word unto those who need to hear it.

Colossians 4:3 *"Withal praying also for us, that God would open unto us a door of utterance, to speak the mystery of Christ, for which I am also in bonds"*

Notice Paul wanted the saints to pray for him that he would open his mouth and make Christ plain to them even though he was in jail. He didn't allow being locked up in jail to cause him to lose focus concerning the open door. He never allowed his bonds or the persecution that he was experiencing to cause him to draw back at all.

Hebrews 10:38,39 *"Now the just shall live by faith: but if any man draw back, my soul shall have no pleasure in him. But we are not of them who draw back unto perdition; but of them that believe to the saving of the soul."*

The Message Bible says, *"It won't be long now, he's on the way; he'll show up most any minute. But anyone who is right with me thrives on loyal trust; if he cuts and runs, I won't be very happy. But we're not quitters who lose out. Oh, no! We'll stay with it and survive, trusting all the way."*

Once we decide to get the word of God out to hurting and dying humanity, Satan will launch an attack against us. He will try to make us run away from the task. We must show the devil that we are going to stay with it. We refuse to make God sad by quitting. But we are going to prove to God that he made the right choice when he entrusted us with this great message. God has given us this opportunity to speak boldly in his name, and we must do it! We must say, "what thus saith the Lord."

Ezekiel 2:6,7,8 *"And thou, son of man, be not afraid of them, neither be afraid of their words, though briers and thorns be with thee, and thou dost dwell among scorpions: be not afraid of their words, nor be dismayed at their looks, though they be a rebellious house. And thou shalt speak my words unto them, whether they will hear, or whether they will forbear: for they are most rebellious. But thou, son of man, hear what I say unto thee; Be not thou rebellious like that rebellious house: open thy mouth, and eat that I give thee."*

THINGS WE MUST DO TO UPGRADE OUR OPEN DOOR

1. SUBMIT TO GOD

James 4:7 *"Submit yourselves therefore to God. Resist the devil, and he will flee from you."*

The Amplified *"So be subject to God. Resist the Devil [stand firm against him], and he will flee from you."*

The Message Bible says, *"So let God work his will in you. Yell a loud no to the Devil and watch him scamper. Say a quiet yes to God and he'll be there in no time."*

2. WALK IN DISCERNMENT

I Kings 3:9 *"Give therefore thy servant an understanding heart to judge thy people, that I may discern between good and bad: for who is able to judge this thy so great a people."*

Solomon in this particular verse is asking God for a hearing heart to judge God's people. He wanted to be able to walk in a level of discernment. He didn't want to call good things evil or evil things good. We definitely need discernment in these times to lead God's people the right way.

Proverbs 8:5 *"O ye simple, understand wisdom: and, ye fools be ye of an understanding heart."*

It is time for us to upgrade our open door by walking in discernment and not live our lives as fools. We need to get wisdom and understanding so we want be deceived by the deception that is in the world around us.

Proverbs 16:2 *"All the ways of a man are clean is his own eyes; but the Lord weigheth the spirits."*

The Message Bible says, *"Humans are satisfied with whatever looks good; God probes for what is good."*

Every believer must be wise enough to know that everything can't be judged by how it appears. We must remember that everything that glitters isn't gold. We must refuse to settle. We must go after only that which God says is good. This will be the wisdom that guides us through the pitfalls of life. It will keep us safe and secure in the arms of our God. This type of understanding will cause us to see what Solomon discovered. He discovered that wisdom is better than money.

Proverbs 16:16 *"How much better is it to get wisdom than gold! and to get understanding rather to be chosen than silver!"*

The Message Bible says, *"Get wisdom—it's worth more than money; choose insight over income every time."*

Proverbs 8:19 *"My fruit is better than gold, yea, than fine gold; and my revenue than choice silver."*

The Message Bible says, *"My benefits are worth more than a big salary, even a very big salary; the returns on me exceed any imaginable bonus."*

3. INVEST

Galatians 6:7,8 *"Be not deceived; God is not mocked: for whatsoever a man soweth, that shall he also reap. For he that soweth to his flesh shall of the flesh reap corruption; but he that soweth to the Spirit shall of the Spirit reap life everlasting."*

The Message Bible says, *"Don't be misled: no one makes a fool of God. What a person plants, he will harvest. The person who plants selfishness, ignoring the needs of others—ignoring God!—harvests a crop of weeds. All he'll have to show for his life is weeds! But the one who plants in response to God, letting God's Spirit do the growth work in him, harvests a crop of real life, eternal life."*

The times in which we live demand that we are sensitive to the needs of others and be willing to invest in the lives of others. We must not be so selfish and indifferent that we fail to invest in the deliverance that so many are crying out to God about. God indeed wants us to be his children who know how to dispense good to others. God will always help our lives go to another level when we help other people's lives improve. He will upgrade the financial doors in our lives as we consider planting good seed into the lives of our neighbor.

These particular scriptures above speak not only of sowing finances, but we can invest love, joy, peace, gentleness, faith, patience and etc. It also includes investing kind words into the lives of others. You and I must be aware of the fact that kind words can heal and bring a breakthrough into someone's life.

Proverbs 15:4 *"A wholesome tongue is a tree of life: but perverseness therein is a breach in the spirit."*

The Message Bible says, *"Kind words heal and help; cutting words wound and maim."*

Many doors will open up for you and I once we invest wholesome words in people's lives. We must upgrade our words to be those that can build

Spiritual Upgrade

up and not tear down. We must not use words that will cut or maim those who are in need of healing. Parents have maimed their children with their words. Children have maimed their parents with their words. Husbands have maimed their wives with their words. Wives have maimed their husbands with their words. We must stop this type of behavior if we truly want God's best. We must fill our mouth with kindness and allow our words to empower and fortify the lives of others before we push someone over the edge. Let's invest words of life and not death.

This is not psychological babble. It is the way believers in Christ must live. We invest ourselves as a seed that goes into the ground and dies. Then it brings forth much more fruit. It truly takes a dying to self to continue to speak kind words to men on a regular basis. It would be a lie to tell you what I'm saying is easy, but you must know it can be done. You and I must walk in the Spirit in order to do it. It will require much self control, but it must be done.

Proverbs 25:28 *"He that hat no rule over his own spirit is like a city that is broken down, and without walls."*

The Message Bible says, *"A person without self-control is like a house with its doors and windows knocked out."*

A Spirit led life is a life that causes us to do what is best for others. The Holy Spirit teaches us to say things and do things to enhance those around us. He guides us this way because he knows the rewards that are involved.

Proverbs 28:10 *"Whoso causeth the righteous to go astray in an evil way, he shall fall himself into his own pit: but the upright shall have good things in possession."*

The Message Bible says, *"Lead good people down a wrong path and you'll come to a bad end; do good and you'll be rewarded for it."*

This is not the time to render evil towards people, but it's time to treat people like they are jewels of the earth. We must treat them like they have greatness written all over them. We must not give in to bad people, but allow them to have to give in to us. This is exactly what our First Black President and his wife did. President Barack Obama and his wife chose to run their campaign in a positive way instead of a negative way.

We must strive to keep ourselves from being polluted. In spite of the evil and corruption around us, we must not give in to functioning at a low level. God has beautified our lives with his power and love and he doesn't want us to allow anyone or anything to stink up our lives.

Proverbs 25:26 says, *"A righteous man falling down before the wicked is as a troubled fountain, and a corrupt spring."*

The Message Bible says, *"A good person who gives in to a bad person is a muddied spring, a polluted well."*

God in these verses is trying to teach us to be the bigger person. He is trying to show us how to take the high road. It is the corrupt nature of man that causes him to invest junk in the life of another human being. We should always seek to invest good and honorable things into the heart and lives of others. Our living and words should cause our city or town to flourish.

Proverbs 11:11 *"By the blessing of the upright the city is exalted: but it is overthrown by the mouth of the wicked."*

The Message Bible says, *"When right-living people bless the city, it flourishes; evil talk turns it into a ghost town in no time."*

UPGRADING YOURSELF IN THE PRESENCE OF GOD

Genesis 3:8 *"And they heard the voice of the Lord God walking in the garden in the cool of the day: and Adam and his wife hid themselves from the presence of the Lord God amongst the trees of the garden."*

The first man by the name of Adam and his precious wife hid themselves from the presence of God because they were afraid. Adam knew he had missed the mark. He disobeyed God Almighty and tried to hide among the trees. This is exactly how all of us live in the first Adam. We hide among things that seem to cover up our shame or nakedness. We hide from the thing we truly need the most. We hide from the presence of God. Our sins drive us away and causes us to miss out on the glory of his presence. We not only hide ourselves from his presence, but we also hide everyone who is attached to us. Men who aren't in the presence of God hide their wives and children from the presence of God.

This man Adam, who represented the entire human race, taught us the wrong way to live. He taught men to try to live apart from the presence of God. This type of living is not only unacceptable, but it will only produce death. Adam's son by the name of Cain when he sinned against God went from the presence of God.

Genesis 4:16 *"And Cain went out from the presence of the Lord, and dwelt in the land of Nod, on the east of Eden."*

The word **Nod** means "wandering, vagabond, flight, to be a fugitive, to lament, and to move the head." In other words without the presence of God, you can't find your true self. All you can do is be a man or woman on the run. Cain left the place of sure answers and ran to a place of no answers. He went to a place where all he was doing was wagging his head. Very simply put, he went to a place of <u>confusion</u>. This is exactly what happens to every one of us without the Lord and his presence in our lives. All we do is become more and more confused. We become more confused about ourselves and our purpose. We become more and more confused about what's right and what's wrong. We become more and more confused about who to turn to for strength and hope. We become more and more confused about what's real and what is not real. We find ourselves walking around scratching and wagging our heads month after month and year after year.

The first Adam brought all of us into a state of unrighteousness and uncleanness which caused us to be cut off from the presence of God. God even gave a warning to Aaron and his sons concerning this in the Old Testament.

Leviticus 22:3 *"Say unto them, Whosoever he be of all your seed among generations, that goeth unto the holy things, which the children of Israel hallow unto the Lord, having his uncleanness upon him, that soul shall be cut off from my presence: I am the Lord."*

You and I could never appear before the presence of God without Jesus because of our uncleanness. Jesus, the last Adam went to appear in the presence of God as our High Priest for us. As a result of what he did, we can now offer prayers and praises that are accepted by our Father.

Hebrews 9:24 *"For Christ is not entered into the holy places made with hands, which are the figures of the true; but into heaven itself, now to appear in the presence of God for us"*

We need to accept what Jesus has done for us and stop running from God and upgrade ourselves in the presence of the Lord. Even those of us who are born again must stop running away from God's presence. Jonah was a mighty prophet who ran from the presence of God. He should had been upgrading himself in God's presence by following God's command, but instead he ran from it.

> Jonah 1:3 *"But Jonah rose up to flee unto Tarshish from the presence of the Lord, and went down to Joppa; and he found a ship going to Tarshish: so he paid the fare thereof, and went down into it, to go with them unto Tarshish from the presence of the Lord."*

I want you to notice something that I believe is vitally important in this text. Notice Jonah fled unto Tarshish from the presence of the Lord. The word **Tarshish** means "she will cause poverty, she will shatter, breaking, subjection, and hard." When we leave the presence of God, we will come to poverty. We will be shattered by life. It will crush us and beat us down. The devil and bad decisions will make life hard for us, and we will become a servant of sin. Life without his presence may start out looking and feeling beautiful, but I guarantee you that it will not end up that way.

Jonah went down to Joppa first and found a ship going to Tarshish. The word **Joppa** means "fair to him, beautiful, and to adorn." In other words you will start out looking beautiful and fair, but you will end up with ugly results. Don't be deceived into believing that there is a good life outside of the presence of the Lord. Jonah not only made things ugly or bad for himself, but he also affected the lives of those who were aboard the ship.

Jonah 1:10 *"Then were the men exceedingly afraid, and said unto him, Why hast thou done this? For the men knew that he fled from the presence of the Lord, because he had told them."*

Despite that the men knew Jonah was fleeing from the presence of God, they still tried to row <u>hard</u> and bring the ship to land. Yet they could not because the sea was tempestuous against them.

Jonah 1:13 *"Nevertheless the men rowed hard to bring it to the land; but they could not: for the sea wrought, and was tempestuous against them."*

Life will always be hard when we flee from God's presence. People can try to assist us, but it will be to no avail because until we get on track with God's presence the sea will not cease from raging. Tarshish was the wrong place for Jonah, and it is the wrong place for you and I. Jesus paid a tremendous price to bring us into the presence of the Father and it is time that we upgrade ourselves in it as soon as possible.

It is imperative that we understand how important the presence of God really is to our lives. God is raising up a church or a called out body of believers who truly refuse to go or do anything without the Lord's presence. This is the attitude that the man of God by the name of Moses had.

Exodus 33:15,16 *"And he said unto him, If thy presence go not with me, carry us not up hence. For wherein shall it be known here that I and thy people have found grace in thy sight? is it not in that thou goest with us? so shall we be separated, I and thy people, from all the people that are upon the face of the earth."*

Notice Moses stated that he knew he had found grace in the sight of God along with God's people based upon God's presence going with him. The presence of God can only be experienced by us because of the grace of God. It is the thing that causes us to stand out from all the people upon the face of the earth. The fact that we have been honored by the presence of God is the most powerful thing in the world. It is like having someone you greatly esteem accompany you somewhere. The only difference is that the Lord is ten thousand times better than anyone you could ever think of. He offers you and I so much more than any human being ever could. The psalmist David knew this to be true and prayed these words to God after he had sinned against God with Bathesheba,

Psalm 51:11 *"Cast me not away from thy presence..."*

David was aware of his need for the presence of God. He understood the thing that made him different from other kings in the earth was God's presence. David knew how to enter into the presence of God and he knew how the presence of God had empowered him in the past. In this text he is crying out for an upgrade. He isn't relying on what used to be. He wants to experience the presence of God afresh and continue to abide in it.

You and I must believe that there is another level of God's presence that we can always experience. As men and women are upgrading and updating different areas of their lives, you and I must seek to upgrade ourselves in God's presence. David found how to get into the presence of God and we need to follow his pattern, especially since we know that the blood of Jesus entitles us to it. We should long for the presence of the Lord. We should desire to bask in it and invite others to come into his presence with us.

David understood that there is emptiness inside of man without the presence of God. This is how David felt without the presence of God. His bones felt dry and broken. The passion he had for the presence of God caused him to judge his wrong action and correct it. Living life without the presence of God is to live life as a vagabond. The punishment is more than any man can bear.

God's presence is the only thing that causes us to feel close to him until the day we will see him face to face. Even though Moses was told by God that he couldn't see his face and live, yet God allowed the glory of his presence to pass by Moses. His presence changed Moses because nobody or nothing can stay the same in God's presence. The presence of God will change everything it comes in contact with. This is why we must get in his presence and strive to abide in the presence of the Almighty God.

THREE WAYS TO COME INTO GOD'S PRESENCE

1. *Thanksgiving*

Psalms 95:2 *"Let us come before his presence with thanksgiving, and make a joyful noise unto him with psalms."*

It is impossible to get into the presence of God murmurring and complaining. God expects us to be thankful unto him and bless his holy name. My thanksgiving is an expression of my gratitude and my faith in God to do what he said he would do. Even if God hears complaining from the sinner, he expects thanksgiving from his people.

Psalms 140:13 *"Surely the righteous shall give thanks unto thy name: the upright shall dwell in thy presence."*

The psalmist is saying that our posture should be one of thanksgiving. It doesn't matter how many people are ungrateful around us, we should be thankful. We who have been made righteous should understand that we must have the presence of God with us or else we refuse to go. And we should totally understand that the presence of God shows up in the midst of thanksgiving and praise. We can't afford to fold our arms and keep our mouths closed. We must lift up our hands and open up our mouths and give thanks unto the Lord.

Many believers know this is true, yet we've allowed ourselves to get up in the morning and complain about our children, spouse, job, finances, and etc. This keeps the presence of God away from us and keeps us out of his presence. It is time to thank the Lord in the morning, the noonday, and in the evening. It's time to give the Lord thanks!

2. *Singing*

Psalms 100:2 *"Serve the Lord with gladness: come before his presence with singing."*

Psalms 96:1,2 *"O Sing unto the Lord a new song: sing unto the Lord, all the earth. Sing unto the Lord, bless his name; show forth his salvation from day to day."*

In the midst of dark times and hard times our God will put a song in our mouths that will invite his presence on the scene. The praise and worship team helps bring us before the presence of the Lord with singing. Singing the word is a powerful thing for you and I to do. The Lord sees and hears us singing, and he comes in our midst with power and protection. People get healed and touch not because of the song, but because of God's presence that showed up as we sang the song. The song didn't do it. The presence of God did it. God's presence showed up and sickness couldn't stay in the room!

3. *The right path*

Psalms 16:11 *"Thou wilt show me the path of life: in thy presence is fulness of joy; at thy right hand there are pleasures for evermore."*

I believe that many people don't understand that God has the correct path for us to travel on. Those of us who follow the God ordained path he has already decided for us, will experience life in his presence. Many believers know that they must thank God and sing to get into his presence, but we must also know that we must stay on the right path. Jonah got off the path, and he went from the presence of the Lord. Singing or thanking God on a ship to Tarshish wouldn't have done Jonah any good. He needed to go to Ninevah not Tarshish. Far too many people think that all they have to do is sing and dance. They have to be made aware that you have to be on the right path. If God wants you in Tarboro, you can't be in Chicago and think that you're in the presence of God. You can't go by a feeling. You must know that God has a specific place for you to be. He has a prearranged path mapped out for your life and to be in his presence requires that you know where it is.

Ephesians 2:10 *"For we are his workmanship, created in Christ Jesus unto good works, which God hath before ordained that we should walk in them."*

The Amplified says, *"For we are God's [own] handiwork (His workmanship), recreated in Christ Jesus, [born anew] that we may do those good works which God predestined (planned beforehand) for us [taking paths which He prepared ahead of time], that we should walk in them [living the good life which He prearranged and made ready for us to live]."*

You must be doing the right thing with the right people. You can't be trying to preach when God told you to be a plumber. They may both start with the letter "p", but they are two different things. The path God has for you was created for you before you were born. If you and I follow the right path, we will live the good life. God has already made it ready for us. We have to get into the word of God because it directs us down the right path.

Psalm 119:105 *"Thy word is a lamp unto my feet, and a light unto my path."*

The word of God causes us to see where we are going. It shines in front of us like the headlights of your automobile. As the sun begins to go down, your headlights become more and more important. Even though in most new cars the headlights are on during the day, it is not until the night falls that we truly value them. We know that we can't travel anywhere at night without them. Even so, as things get darker and darker for the world the word of God is what you and I should place more and more value on. It will cause us to navigate through this life successfully.

Proverbs 3:5,6 *"Trust in the Lord with all thine heart; and lean not unto thine own understanding. In all thy ways acknowledge him, and he shall direct thy paths."*

The Message Bible says, *"Trust God from the bottom of your heart; don't try to figure out everything on your own. Listen for God's voice in everything you do, everywhere you go; he's the one who will keep you on track."*

These verses and their translation reveal to us what leads us away from the path that God has ordained for our lives—our own understanding. We try to figure everything out. We make moves and decision based on our limited knowledge. This leads us out of the presence of the Father. We marry the wrong person or we choose the wrong house, car, or job. We aren't aware of how despaerately our Father wants to direct our steps down a chosen path. We fail to listen for the voice of God to bring specific instructions that will bring us into his best. We don't know it all, but he does. We must be governed or controlled by the principles set forth in God's word.

Proverbs 11:4 *"Riches profit not in the day of wrath: but righteousness delivered from death."*

The Message Bible says, *"A thick bankroll is no help when life falls apart, but a principled life can stand up to the worst."*

WHAT DOES THE PRESENCE OF GOD DO FOR US?

1. The presence of God hides you from the pride of men

Psalm 31:20 *"Thou shalt hide them in the secret of thy presence from the pride of man: thou shalt keep them secretly in a pavilion from the strife of tongues."*

Everyone of us must attest to the fact that we live in a very ungodly society. This automatically means that you and I will have our share of haters. Only God can hide you in a place where men can't get to you. He will protect you from the very hatred in their mouths. He will cause you to be in a pavilion. A pavilion is a large tent raised on posts. It is a part of a building higher and more decorated than the rest. In other words, God is saying, "When you get in my presence, I will put you in a high place." God is saying that he will put you in a place that looks better than anything you've ever seen before in your life. A pavilion is also one of a group of buildings forming a hospital. This means that God will give you total recovery from all the hurtful words of men. He will keep you safe in his Spiritual Intensive Care Unit. He will keep you safe from the negative words of men until you get full restoration. He will nurse you back to health with his holy presence.

The carnal man full of pride may think he will destroy you the same way he has destroyed others, but he doesn't know that God's presence won't allow him to find you. I've seen him do it for me, and I know he will do it for you.

2. The presence of God will cause wicked men to perish

Psalm 37:20 *"But the wicked shall perish, and the enemies of the Lord shall be as the fat of lambs: they shall consume; into smoke shall they consume away."*

Psalm 68:2 *"As smoke is driven away, so drive them away: as wax melteth before the fire, so let the wicked perish at the presence of God.*

These two verses divinely point out to you and I the power of God's presence. They reveal to us that God's presence will not support the wicked but rather it will consume them. Those who have been charging you astronomical prices for things or seeking to take advantage of you in your wages will be dealt with by the presence of God. We've got to believe that God's presence will drive them away like smoke. God will drive away anything that man is trying to suffocate in your life. He will blow them out of the way and cause you to <u>breathe in the air of increase</u>.

3. The presence of God causes stuff to shake, move, melt, and tremble

Psalm 68:8 *"The earth shook, the heavens also dropped at he presence of God: even Sinai itself was moved at the presence of God, the God of Israel."*

Psalms 97:5 *"The hills melted like wax at the presence of the Lord, at the presence of the Lord of the whole earth."*

Psalm 114:7,8 *"Tremble, thou earth, at the presence of the Lord, at the presence of the God of Jacob; which turned the rock into a standing water, the flint into a fountain of waters."*

Isaiah 64:1,2,3 *"Oh that thou wouldest rend the heavens, that thou wouldest come down, that the mountains might flow down at thy presence, as when the melting fire burneth, the fire causeth the waters to boil, to make thy name known to thine adversaries, that the nations may tremble at thy presence! When thou didst terrible things which we looked not for, thou camest down, the mountains flowed down at thy presence."*

Nahum 1:5 *"The mountains quake at him, and the hills melt, and the earth is burned at his presence, yea, the world, and all that dwell therein."*

All of the above verses you've just read prove a profound fact, that nothing stands still in the presence of God. God's presence will always shift stuff around in your life. This is why the enemy doesn't want you to praise or magnify the Lord. He knows that something is going to shake besides you. This speaks of the total awesomeness of his presence. He is the only one that can melt mountains like little candles by his presence. He is the only one that can cause mountains to tremble with his presence. Therefore, every time you are giving God the glory in the house of God or at your home expect to see other things move out of your way as well. There is no way you can radically praise our God with your whole heart and see the same results year after year. Something will change in the presence of our God. Big things will become small and melt away in the presence of our King!

4. The presence of God brings times of refreshing

Acts 3:19 *"Repent ye therefore, and be converted, that your sins may be blotted out, when the times of refreshing shall come from the presence of the Lord"*

The Amplified says, *"So repent (change your mind and purpose), turn around and return [to God], that your sins may be erased (blotted out, wiped clean), that times of refreshing (of recovering from the effects of heat, of reviving with fresh air) may come from the presence of the Lord."*

The Message Bible says, *"Now it's time to change your ways! Turn to face God so he can wipe away your sins, pour out showers of blessing to refresh you."*

Many of us have been through things that we had to recover from. We can never get use to losing a love one unexpectedly. I've seen people in the congregation that I pastor have to endure this type of incident and the only thing that brought them through it was the presence of God. His presence is the only thing that brought them through this type of situation. It wasn't the preacher's sermon that took away their tears. It was the presence of God that showed up in a song or a poem. God's presence must show up in the room and cause preaching to be made easy. A room that doesn't carry his presence will not revive people from this type of pain. When a daughter loses her dad or mother, it is a pain that cuts deep into her soul. The presence of God will come into the room and pour out blessings of peace that is beyond human understanding.

This is one of the main reasons why God calls man to a place of repentance, so man can enjoy the presence of God once again. Every crisis you've been through or traumatic experience will never be greater than the presence of God. Don't let sin make you miss out on the showers of blessings that God wants to pour out on you. Change your ways and turn your face to God so he can blow fresh wind upon your life. This is an open opportunity that you and I can't afford to miss. This is the day you've been waiting for and God has set it up just for you. The presence of men can only comfort you for a brief moment, but God's presence will walk you through things that will blow your mind. Many of us can truly say that God can refresh you through tough times. He'll be there with the main thing you need—His Presence!

5. The presence of God brings rest and peace

Exodus 33:14 *"And he said, My presence shall go with thee, and I will give thee rest."*

These potent words spoken to Moses still bring comfort to my soul today. I believe anxiety and stress can't be fully overcome by a tablet or medicine. I believe that the root of stress is a lack of dependence on the presence of God. Far too many of us try to handle things on our own. We have to depend on the presence of God once again. The presence of God will bring you to a place of peace. You don't have to fear when you know the Lord is going with you. The saints of old used to sing a little song that said, "Where he leads me I will follow." The desire of our hearts is never to go without the Lord. It is too dangerous and unsure. The only sure way to know victory will take place is when he goes with us. This is our peace in the midst of every battle that we face. The Lord is with us whithersoever we go!

6. The presence of God brings the anointing and power

Luke 5:17 *"And it came to pass on a certain day, as he was teaching, that there were Pharisees and doctors of the law sitting by, which were come out of every town of Galilee, and Judaea, and Jerusalem: and the power of the Lord was present to heal them."*

I along with many other great leaders of our day can't even begin to articulate in words how grateful we are that the presence of God shows up in our midst and heals the sick. The anointing of God is still amazing to watch in action. It can still cause every disease that the devil has put on man to be taken off them in an instant. The true sign of the anointing showing up in our midst is that the sick will be healed. Everywhere Jesus went the sick were healed. This is why we spend time in prayer. We desire to see the power of the Lord present to heal the people who are suffering in their bodies.

God wants us to know this type of power in a new way. We must empty ourselves of all dependence on our flesh to do anything in the supernatural. We must believe that the anointing or power of God will confirm the teaching of his word with powerful demonstrations of healing. Notice Jesus is teaching among some of the greatest minds of his day. The Pharisees and doctors of law may have only come out for teaching, but the presence of God gave them something more. Today, the extra thing that the people need can only be found in the anointing. God wants us to welcome his presence in our midst so that he can move mightily among us. He wants to heal every individual of every sickness and disease. We must make room for it to happen in our local assembly.

7. The presence of God causes the prophetic to be released

I Samuel 10:5,6,7 *"After that thou shalt come to the hill of God, where is the garrison of the Philistines: and it shall come to pass, when thou art come thither to the city, that thou shalt meet a company of prophets coming down from the high place with a psaltery, and a tabret, and a pipe, and a harp, before them; and they shall prophesy: And the spirit of the Lord will come upon thee, and thou shalt prophesy with them; and they shall prophesy: And the spirit of the Lord will come upon thee, and thou shalt prophesy with them, and shalt be turned into another man. And let it be, when these signs are come unto thee, that thou do as occasion serve thee; for God is with thee."*

I think it is so important in this time that we learn to move in the prophetic arena with deep sensitivity. I think we fail to emphasize how important the presence of God is to the prophetic. The verse you just read speaks of the fact that the whole company of prophets were coming down from the high place with psaltery, tabret, pipe, and harp. These prophets have musical instruments before them because they understand the importance of the presence of God to the prophetic arena. Wherever real worship and praise is being released there will be a strong prophetic utterance. One of the greatest prophets in our Bible was David. God truly wants us to speak forth his heart and mind to encourage the spirits of men and women. This is not out of the realm of the flesh, but the presence of God will give birth to radical utterances that the mind can't even fathom. These prophetic words will come because we valued God's presence. The Spirit of the Lord will cause men who thought about throwing in the towel to hear the word of the Lord and live again.

This is why we must upgrade ourselves in God's presence among those who are moving in his presence afresh. We need musical instruments in the hands of prophetic people. I think we must allow his presence to release people out of their comfort zone into a spiritual dimension of the kingdom of God where there is nothing but wholeness.

8. The presence of God brings the goodness of God

Exodus 33:19 *"And he said, I will make all my goodness pass before thee; and will be gracious to whom I will be gracious, and will show mercy on whom I will show mercy."*

Have you ever noticed when God's presence truly shows up in the midst of a service that you partake of God's goodness in a whole new way? When we truly enter into the presence of God, we say that the Lord

Spiritual Upgrade

---

is good not as a cliché. The goodness of God starts to be something that is so real to you that you actually feel that you can taste it. It becomes so powerful and you start to see how gracious God can be to you. When his goodness shows up, you start to expect to see the goodness of the Lord in the land of the living. You know that his mercy is in your midst. It is at this time that you will begin to cry because you know he has been so good to you that you will never be able to repay him. Even if God allowed me to live another thousand years, I couldn't begin to thank him enough for his mercy and grace. His presence is so good, and it is so good to be in his presence. The presence of God brings good things in the spirit realm and the natural realm. His goodness has everything in it that a man or woman can ever need or desire. When his goodness shows up in the room, people start stretching out on the floor. They start bowing down and weeping profusely. They can hardly leave the building. I've seen his goodness hold people in worship for hours after the service was ended. These moments make you know with all assurance that there is nobody like our God. His presence that carries his goodness will cause you to lift your hands in spontaneous worship and adoration. You start to discern where his grace brought you from and where he is taking you next. It is his goodness that overwhelms you and causes you to look at everything you have gone through or been through as light affliction.

Every year for the past few years my brother and I along with several other bishops and pastors from our area and the Raleigh area go on a retreat. This is an enlightening experience for us as pastors. We spend time worshipping and praying concerning our own lives and ministries. There have been times when the worship was so strong that we lingered around while the psalmist played the piano. The goodness of God filled the atmosphere, and we felt as if we couldn't leave. The presence of God had us for that period of time, and we didn't care. His goodness was passing by and showing up with everything we needed. We didn't see his face, but we had his presence.

9. The presence of God brings the fullness of joy

Psalm 16:11 *"Thou wilt show me the path of life: in thy presence is fulness of joy; at thy right hand there are pleasures for evermore."*

The Message Bible says, *"Now you've got my feet on the life path, all radiant from the shining of your face. Ever since you took my hand, I'm on the right way."*

The God you serve wants you to walk in joy. He takes no delight in seeing his children depressed. He has chosen us to rule, and it is impossible to reign in life without joy. The presence of God brings laughter and joy like we have never experienced. This joy brings with it a renewed energy. It causes us to stand.

I can recall so vividly when I first got saved and would attend services as a young lad in Christ how the presence of God brought such joy into my life that

Spiritual Upgrade

I knew I could bubble over anything. The joy that he brought was unexplainable. I remember feeling odd because I was happy about everything. It was easy to give thanks in everything because the joy of God's presence was upon me. I could hardly go to sleep because of the joy of his presence. This joy carried me to church, to work, to my home, and to bed. That was many years ago, and it is still just as powerful in my life today. It is still my strength.

It is at this time that you need to stay away from those who know very little about the joy of God's presence because they will make you think it is a phase you are going through. They will tell you that this will come to an end, and you will settle down. They fail to prove it by the scriptures. This is not a feeling; this is the dynamic of God's presence. As long as you upgrade yourself in God's presence, the joy will not depart. Many of us who walk in this type of joy are so blessed by it. Don't believe the lie of the enemy when he tries to make you think that being down is normal for the believer. It is normal for the believer to walk in the joy of the Lord's presence.

This type of joy will cause you to live above feelings and circumstances of your day. The circumstances don't tell us when to be happy. God tells us to trust him and count it all joy. He has everything under the authority of his word, and I believe the word. I can truly say that I have never seen my brother (Wayne), my sister (Susan), or my mother down since they have been saved. This doesn't mean that they haven't had a chance to be down, but they have learned to refuse to be down. They are being carried by the joy of God's presence.

Jude verse 24 *"Now unto him that is able to keep you from falling, and to present you faultless before the presence of his glory with exceeding joy"*

Psalm 105:43 *"And he brought forth his people with joy, and his chosen with gladness"*

10. The presence of God brings angelic assistance

Daniel 3:28 *"Then Nebuchadnezzar spake, and said, Blessed be the God of Shadrach, Meshach, and Abed-nego, who hath sent his angel, and delivered his servants that trusted in him, and have changed the king's word, and yielded their bodies, that they might not serve nor worship any god, except their own God.*

Psalm 34:7 *"The angel of the Lord encampeth round about them that fear him, and delivered them."*

God will assist you and me with angelic help as we walk in his presence. Sometimes we fail to acknowledge this part of our covenant rights because we don't always see these powerful spirits that are on our side. We who hearken unto the voice of God's word will have their assistance as we seek to do our Father's will. They will stand guard over our lives when we face dangerous situations.

11. The presence of God brings supernatural intelligence

This is one of the most exciting things about getting into the presence of God. The presence of God causes you and I to think on a whole new level. This is why people who walk in the presence of God always seem to have very creative ideas, thoughts, and sayings. They didn't get them from their natural mind. None of King Solomon's proverbs came from man's carnal thinking. God blessed this man with supernatural wisdom and insight. God's insights and wisdom is what causes great rulers and kings to rule, and it will be there for you and I as we enter into his presence. These insights will cause those who hear thee to be blessed or empowered in ways they never thought possible.

Proverbs 8:6,15,16 *"Hear; for I will speak of excellent things; and the opening of my lips shall be right things. By me kings reign, and princes decree justice. By me princes rule, and nobles, even all the judges of the earth.*

This type of spiritual intelligence also includes walking in the morality outlined in the word. I believe that we can't afford to have intelligence that leaves out living a godly life. Natural intelligence fails to make us all we need to be because it leaves out the counsel of God. This is why we make so many bad choices with all our so called smarts.

> "To educate a man in mind and not in morals is to educate a menace to society."
> **Theodore Roosevelt** (26th President)

These eleven things make the presence of God vital to every individual. His presence provides the protection that we need. Many of us know of incidents in our lives where the only thing that got us out safely was the presence of God. His presence contains everything that he is and everything he has. There is no want or lack in his presence. We must totally sell out to the fact that we die outside of his presence and can only live in his presence. We must never allow anyone to cut us off from the presence of the Lord. A baby inside of his mother's womb breathes as a result of his connection to the cord, so do we breathe and exist because of our connection to God. We must once again upgrade ourselves in the presence of God and tap into this spiritual understanding. Notice what is stated in Jude verse 24 from another translation:

The Message Bible says, *"And now to him who can keep you on your feet, standing tall in his bright presence, fresh, and celebrating—to our one God, our only Savior, through Jesus Christ, our Master, be glory, majesty, strength, and rule before all time, and now and to the end of all time. Yes."*

UPGRADING YOUR SPIRITUAL SENSITIVITY
(CHECKING YOUR SPIRITUAL REFLEXES)

Those of us who go to the doctor to get a physical know how important it is to have good reflexes. The doctor who enters the room will take his medical reflex hammer and gently tap your knees. He does this because he wants to make sure that your reflexes are working properly. He knows that our reflexes are not controlled by our own will. They are a direct response to a stimulation of sensory nerve cells. Our reflexes are not voluntary. In other words if you try not to respond to the tap that he gives to a certain place on your knee it would be to no avail. Mainly because you have no control over whether or not you respond it is a reflex reaction to the tap on that certain spot. You can't help it.

I believe our time in the presence of God and in prayer will cause us to receive heavenly stimulation that will send a spiritual signal to our spiritual nerve cells and we can't help but respond. Those of us who have spent time in his presence and with the Lord walk in a sensitivity to the voice of God and spiritual things. If God can show up in the sanctuary and you feel absolutely nothing or you can go to sleep, then you need a check up. If he can deliver people from terminal illnesses and you do not get excited, you need a checkup. If he can allow your church to raise money to send missionaries to Africa or some other part of the world and you aren't moved, you need a check up. If people can be delivered from bondages that once had them bound and you feel nothing at all, you need a spiritual check up. Something is wrong with your spiritual reflexes.

The word <u>*sensitive*</u> is defined as receiving impressions readily. I believe that time in the presence of God and his word will cause you to receive impressions from heaven on a regular basis. You and I should be men and women of God who are always anxious to receive the word of the Lord. We should always be anxious or excited about seeing God's power come in our midst.

Psalm 63:1,2 *"O God, thou art my God; early will I seek thee: my soul thirsteth for thee, my flesh longeth for thee in a dry and thirsty land, where no water is; To see thy power and thy glory, so as I have seen thee in the sanctuary."*

David was a man who was very sensitive to God. He was longing to see God's power and glory. He was broken and full of contrition. I believe God wants us reaching out to him like this today and being sensitive to the impressions he makes upon our hearts and mind. He wants us to go when he tells us to go and to move when he tells us to move. Our testimony must not be like Jacob who fell asleep in Haran and had no idea that the Lord was in the place.

> Genesis 28:16,17 *"And Jacob awaked out of his sleep, and he said, Surely the Lord is in this place; and I knew it not."*

I think far too many believers live like Jacob. We should be so alive to God that the devil can't stand our guts. Every time he sees us coming he begins to tremble because he should know here comes a believer who is sensitive to God. We operate like elder brother Jesus instead of Jacob. Jacob was afraid of the move of God. He was afraid of what God showed him.

> Genesis 28:17 *"And he was afraid, and said, How dreadful is this place! This is none other but the house of God, and this is the gate of heaven."*

We must not be afraid to act on what God is telling us. We must hearken diligently to God's voice. This is why we can't afford to be drunk with foolish jesting and other things that will steal our sensitivity to God. A drunk man who has taken in too much alcohol will give little or no response to the stimulation around him. He is numb to the things going on around him. He sees and feels absolutely nothing. His nerve cells are affected by the alcohol in his body.

Let me ask you a question, "When worship songs are going forth about the blood and your Lord, do you feel anything?" You should because you know his blood washed away your sins. You should enjoy what the sinner can't comprehend because he is dead to your world and you are dead to his.

You and I will never be successful in the kingdom if we are not spiritually sensitive. I believe your spiritual sensitivity will cause you to deal successfully with every area of your life. Most of us are far too sensitive in the natural than we are in the spirit. This must change. We must upgrade our sensitivity and reflexes before it is too late. The voice of God is too important.

UPGRADING YOUR HEALTH AND RELATIONSHIPS

These next two areas that I will strive to touch are vital to your life. Many times because so little value and attention are given to these areas, Satan seems to set up his workshop in them. He wants us to continue to die these untimely deaths and blame God for our negligence. I believe our Heavenly Father is raising up men and women in the body of Christ with great insights in these areas so that we might put the devil in check and upgrade our lives.

Psalms 91:16 *"With long life will I satisfy him..."*

God has plainly stated to us in his word that he will satisfy us with long life. However, this particular promise is being lost by many believers in the body of Christ, because of our refusal to make serious and definite changes or upgrades in our health. So many of us haven't taken personal responsibility in this

Spiritual Upgrade

---

area, and it is costing us dearly. I believe as we have upgraded our phones and television, if we are going to be around to use these things, we must upgrade our health. You and I must examine the kinds of foods that we are putting in our bodies and our exercise regiment. Our parents and grandparents may have eaten certain things because they couldn't afford to buy healthy foods. You and I must recognize that we are more important or valuable than any gadget that man can create. Our health is worth the price.

I remember years ago when we invited Dr. Calvin Ellison, pastor of Oasis of Hope in Farmville, to our church to talk to our people about healthy eating. I warned them that once we heard the truth we would be responsible for carrying it out.

James 4:17 *"Therefore to him that knoweth to do good, and doeth it not, to him it is sin."*

This is a divine principle that we must respect. Once we are made aware of something that is wholesome for our lives we are obligated to carry it forth. I knew many of the things Dr. Ellison would present to us would challenge us. And this is exactly what he did. I personally had a love for hog chitterlings. My grandfather ate hog chitterlings. My father ate hog chitterlings and my mother ate hog chitterlings. In fact my mother-in-law before she died would clean and cook hog chitterlings for me every Thanksgiving. She would prepare turkey, potato salad, greens, and <u>hog chitterlings</u> just for me. I used to look forward to it. She would clean them so well, believe it or not,

Spiritual Upgrade

that you couldn't even smell the bad odor that chitterlings have. They were well seasoned and cooked to the delight of my taste buds.

Plus, there were certain restaurants in Tarboro where I used to purchase them. I would buy some at least once every week. Yet one of the main things that Dr. Calvin Ellison talked to us about was eating hog chitterlings. I received the word and vowed to my church that I wouldn't eat them again. I knew if I would openly say it in front of the flock that I would be able to overcome eating them. I haven't eaten any since. You might ask the question, "Bishop Sharpe, do you ever desire to eat hog chitterlings?" My honest answer to you would be "Yes, but I value my health." I desire to live a victorious life in every area of my life, and I know I can't do it with bad eating habits.

Another thing that I used to thoroughly enjoy was sodas. I loved every kind of soda, but especially Mountain Dew, Pepsi, and Grape. My grandparents, uncles, aunts, nieces, and cousins have always drank sodas as far as I can remember. Sodas were always a part of every family reunion or any eating event. At my home, I can remember drinking sodas for breakfast, lunch and dinner. My daughter and I loved them. It was nothing for me to drink three or four sodas a day. Before Dr. Ellison came, I had cut back to about two per day. I thought that was pretty good; however, through his teaching I saw how devastating these things were to my life. My wife and I made a commitment to no longer drink sodas. It is the last thing we ever look for at an eating event. I also noticed

Spiritual Upgrade

to my surprise that once I gave up sodas, I started to like water. While I was drinking sodas, I didn't drink much water. I would drink little or no water, but once I gave up sodas, water started to taste better. Today I love and enjoy water. I also noticed that once I gave up sodas, people started offering them to me everywhere I went. Even today it seems like everywhere I go someone is always offering me a soda to drink. When I used to drink them, they didn't seem to be as readily available to me. This tells me two things that the devil wants us dead and that most people that are around us today drink sodas. I have met far too many Christians who state to me that they drink tea, kool aid, or sodas, but little or no water. This leads to all kinds of health problems. We can totally destroy our bladder. We've got to change.

Let me make myself very clear that this section of the book is to exhort or urge you to eat healthy, but it is not designed to condemn you or to analyze you. I am plainly stating that you must make some upgrades in the health area so you can get the most out of your body. This upgrade must also include walking and exercising. I believe that we as believers must become more active. I am not talking about trying to be a body builder or a super model. I am talking about walking and exercising to have a healthy heart. Many of us can honestly say we have treadmills, bicycles, and other exercise equipment that we rarely use. This must change. Our time has come for us to break a sweat doing something in the area of exercise. We must walk or run on the treadmill and admonish our brothers and sisters to do the same. This will require

Spiritual Upgrade

discipline, but in the end we will feel better. More importantly, we will be in better shape. Again, I am not trying to be a health expert or a health fanatic, but rather admonish you to become more health conscious. We must remember we serve a good God who wants us to be in good health.

I believe another area often overlooked as it relates to our health is the area of <u>rest</u>. Many times we as believers try to be effective at what we've been assigned to do without resting our bodies properly. This puts us at a disadvantage to Satan. Many great preachers and teachers of the gospel fail to get eight hours of rest that is necessary to replenish our bodies. We seem to act like we believe it is a sin to rest, but it is not. Without the proper amount of sleep, we become grouchy and indifferent. We are easily angered and behave in a way that doesn't glorify our Lord.

I know what some people are saying as they read this part of the book. You are saying, you don't need that much sleep, but the real truth of the matter is that we do. It is unhealthy for us to keep trying to stay up twenty hours and only rest four hours. This is why so many of us go to sleep in the house of God. It is not because the sermon is boring. It's because we didn't go to bed at an appropriate time the night before.

Some great men and women have even pushed themselves into an heart attack because of a lack of rest. Jesus understood the importance of rest when he walked this earth. He rested in the hinder part of ships. He also pulled his disciples aside, so they could get some rest.

St. Mark 6:31 *"And he said unto them, Come ye yourselves apart into a desert place, and rest a while: for there were many coming and going, and they had no leisure so much as to eat."*

You and I must go to a place each day and night away from every crowd or noise and rest our bodies. I strive each day to always get my rest. I don't leave it up to others because people are always wanting or needing you for something. I recognize that sharp pains start shooting through my head if I don't get enough rest. I'm not able to function at my highest level when I haven't rested properly. I also thank God that I have preachers around me who also admonish me to get my rest. You and I need these type of people around us because your care and concern for others will cause you to misuse your body. Without proper care of your body, you will destroy everything the Father wants to do through you. There is much more I could say about this area, but I hope and pray you got the point.

I wish to also point out to you that part of being able to rest your body properly is being able to rest your mind. This can only be done two ways. The first way is making sure you think **good thoughts**. You must make a decision to refuse to think negative about your life and others. You must think about those things that add to who you are and not those things that take away from who you are. In order to do this, you will have to be very diligent towards the things of God. You will have to make a daily attempt

Spiritual Upgrade

to guard and protect your mind against toxic thoughts that steal from your life.

This is why you can't afford to watch a bunch of scary movies containing rape, violence, and murder. You must think about things that connect with the goodness of God. You must think about things that cause you to see the good in others and the world in which you live. Your good thoughts will take your life to a whole new level.

The second way to rest your mind is by having a **hobby** or **doing something that relaxes you**. I truly enjoy playing solitaire on the computer. I find it very relaxing. I also enjoy watching a good television show with my wife or a good movie. This is why some enjoy the game of golf, fishing, reading, or etc. You must do something that causes your mind and body to rest. You have to recognize you can't live in a tense mood on a twenty four hour basis and expect your body to function effectively for you. You must do some thing that is pleasurable for you. It can't be about your husband, the kids, or the in-laws. This must be something you like doing. If you are a husband, it can't be about your wife at this time. You must find something you enjoy and do it in order to put your mind and body at ease. In my younger years I would go to the gym and play full court basketball. However, as time and years past, you must upgrade your hobbies to fit where you are. It is no longer feasible for many people to play basketball or baseball anymore, but you can play it on your X box or the Wii game. My wife and I enjoy playing tennis and bowling on the Wii. For those who really have energy

Spiritual Upgrade

to burn, you should try boxing on the Wii game. It will definitely relax your mind, but your arms and body will be exhausted. Again, I am only tossing out a few things that I do to relax my mind. Yours might be totally different. You might enjoy swimming, chess, or something else. It doesn't matter as long as you rest your mind with a godly hobby.

The next area I will strive to help us upgrade is our relationship. I believe the older you get the more value you should place on the relationships the Father has allowed you to develop. These are so special and have to be updated all the time. The devil has so many people valuing stuff that they fail to care anything at all about the people they are coming in contact with. I don't believe you should take relationships for granted. Many of us seem to value people so little while they are alive. Still, I have noticed that some of us are choosing our relationships based on material things. This has nothing to do with spirituality. We tend to believe what we have entitles us to hang around some people and disqualifies us to hang around others. We start measuring ourselves the same way the world measures us. We must upgrade our relationships and decide to call and keep in contact with people who have been a blessing to us along the way.

I have friends whose churches own several acres of property, and I have friends who are in store front buildings. Some are still renting, but their relationship is still important to my life. They have spoken prophecies over my life that I know are accurate. I believe in them, and they believe in me. I value them,

Spiritual Upgrade

---

and they value me. It has nothing to do with the material realm. It is bigger than that. These people know and love God and that's important to me.

Many times because of your schedule you can't call or talk to these people everyday or every week. However, when you do talk or see these special persons it's as if you haven't skipped a beat. The relationship is still in tact and you feel such love and compassion for them and the assignment on their lives. Several of my relationships come to mind as I write this manuscript. I will only mention three for time's sake. I don't see any of them everyday nor do I call any of them every week. Yet, these people are so special to God and I totally value who they are in the body of Christ. The first person I think about is Pastor Kenneth Anderson who pastors God of Deliverance in Rocky Mount, N.C. I don't see him everyday and we don't talk on the phone every week. He is a man who definitely loves the Lord and a great friend. The second person who comes to mind is Bishop Rosie O'Neal who pastors Koinonia Church in Greenville, N.C. She is a powerful woman of God who has a tremendous heart for God's people. And the third person is Dr. Mal Williams who pastors United Fellowship Assembly in Nashville, N.C. He is an awesome singer and preacher in the body of Christ. I remember years ago I asked God why did I feel so close to these people and I haven't been around them everyday nor seen them. I heard the Lord speak plainly to my heart. He said, "Because you haven't spoken anything evil about these people behind their back nor have they you. Therefore, when you see each other you haven't skipped a beat from the last time you were with them." This was an eye opener and confirmation to my spirit. You see true relationships speak well of each other in their presence and in their absence.

The ones that are not real will utter bad things about you behind your back. They usually can't look you in your face when they see you. You will not be able to connect with them no matter how hard you try. The negative words being uttered by them about you behind your back causes an invisible wall to be built. They don't desire to see you succeed. You and I must upgrade our relationship with people who truly desire to see us do well.

Again, I could have mentioned many, many friends or men and women of God, but I mention these for time's sake. The point that I am trying to cause you to grasp is that God wants you to focus on your relationships more than your buildings, cars, houses, land, and money. I believe <u>one of the reasons</u> God has allowed man to create the cell phone, fax, e-mail, internet, and etc. is to *harness and protect relationships*. There is no reason we can't build and cultivate relationships in the kingdom of God.

I believe what I enjoy just as much as seeing people delivered is the relationships that I've made as I have preached in different cities and states. Some people just want to preach and go back to the hotel or go home. I personally enjoy fellowshipping with the Set Man or Set Woman of God and greeting those who I've been given an opportunity to minister to. I enjoy hearing their stories and testimonies of how the word of God blessed them or some of the things God has worked out for them. God's people are special people. And I believe if you don't care about people you will never be promoted by God because he only gives us position and power for the purpose of blessing people.

We should use those free cell phone minutes to give our friends and family a call, especially your spouse and children. They deserve this upgrade because of all the sacrifices they have made for you. Let's use those free weekend minutes and after 7p.m or after 9p.m. minutes to give someone you love a call, before you allow a good relationship to die.

It's time for a spiritual upgrade to take place in the area of your covenant relationships. You must continue to value every relationship that is promoting you to be a better saint of the Most High God. Make them aware of their value to you. Let them know that you don't believe it is a seasonal thing between you and them. Love them with an everlasting love—the agape of God!

UPGRADING YOUR FOCUS
LOOKING AHEAD

It is important for every believer in Christ to understand one of the enemy's main tactics that he uses to keep our lives from moving forward is distraction. Our adversary tries to distract us. He wants our eyes off the future blessings our Heavenly Father has established for us in the earth. Those of us who are heeding the sound of the trumpet haven't lost our focus. We recognize that distracted minds and hearts never get the prize. They never reach their destination or accomplish their dreams.

Focused people, on the other hand, are relentless. They are full of determination and resolve. Focused people don't allow themselves to be distracted by the problems or negative situations of their day. They understand that the solution is in front of them as long as they keep their eyes on Jesus.

Hebrews 12:2 *"Looking unto Jesus the author and finisher of our faith: who for the joy that was set before him endured the cross, despising the shame, and is set down at the right hand of the throne of God."*

The Amplified says, *"Looking away [from all that will distract] to Jesus, Who is the Leader and the Source of our faith [giving the first incentive for our belief] and is also its Finisher [bringing it to maturity and perfection]. He, for the joy [of obtaining the prize] that was set before Him, endured the cross, despising and ignoring the shame, and is now seated at the right hand of the throne of God."*

Notice these verses are admonishing us to pay close attention to how Jesus succeeded. It is exhorting us to remember this story, so we can plow through what we face. The example of Jesus will shoot adrenaline through your soul. It will cause you to look ahead for the exhilarating finish that awaits you.

The word **distract** means "to draw away the mind or attention." The enemy is always trying to show us something that will move our mind or thought away from Jesus Christ. He knows as long as our eyes are on the Lord, we can see supernatural things take place. The Apostle Peter was able to walk on water as long as his eyes were on Jesus, but when he focused on the wind, he began to sink.

Matthew 14:28,29,30 says, *"And Peter answered him and said, Lord, If it be thou, bid me come unto thee on the water. And he said, Come. And when Peter was come down out of the ship, he walked on the water, to go to Jesus. But when he saw the wind boisterous, he was afraid; and beginning to sink., he cried, saying, Lord, save me."*

These verses show us that looking at strong winds instead of Jesus will always lead to a downward spiral. It is when we focus on the Lord that our lives begin to go upward. I believe it is very important for us to know that this is not a time to look to the White House or our government for all the answers we need. Looking at what is going on in the economy will only cause fear to arise. Looking at the unemployment rate will only cause fear to arise. We must focus our attention on Jesus and the supernatural power of God. Let's look at these verses in another Bible translation.

The Message Bible says, *"Peter, suddenly bold, said, "Master, if it's really you, call me to come to you on the water." He said, "Come ahead." Jumping out of the boat, Peter walked on the water to Jesus. But when he looked down at the waves churning beneath his feet, he lost his nerve and started to sink. He cried, "Master, save me!"*

Those of us who have allowed our eyes to be taken off him must refocus them once again. This is exactly what Peter did. He cried out to the Lord and walked back to the ship with his focus in place. The

Spiritual Upgrade

Bible tells us that the wind didn't stop blowing until they returned to the ship.

Matthew 14:32 *"And when they were come into the ship, the wind ceased."*

This verse causes us to understand that being focused doesn't stop the wind but it does stop your fears. People who are focused remain in faith. They still believe God in the midst of the storms of life. They keep looking ahead because they see the joy that is set before them. They continue to upgrade their focus on a daily, weekly, monthly, and yearly basis. They don't turn to the left or to the right but they look straight ahead at the things God said in his law. They know that focused people are winning people!

UPGRADING YOURSELF IN EXCELLENCE

The word <u>excellence</u> means "high quality or being better than others." **Quality** is defined as *something special about an object that makes it what it is*. It means "fineness or merit." It is with these definitions in line that we will strive to upgrade ourselves.

"I believe the destiny of your generation—and your nation—is a rendezvous with excellence."
Lyndon B. Johnson (36th President)

I definitely agree with this statement as it relates to our spiritual life and natural life. Those of us in the body of Christ must believe that we are to strive to do the Lord's business with excellence.

I believe in being on time for doctor appointments, weddings, and etc., but I also believe in being on time for the house of God. I don't think we can always tell when our services are going to end, but we know when they will start. Again, I remind you

Spiritual Upgrade

that this book is striving to get you to upgrade your spiritual life. This means that we should be patient with the clock at the house of God the same way we are when it comes to a natural visit at the doctor's office. For example, you may have an appointment with your doctor or dentist at 10'oclock in the morning but may not be asked by the secretary to come in the back until 10:45 a.m. Once you are taken to be weighed, you will probably spend another ten or fifteen minutes waiting in the room for the doctor to come in. Finally, the doctor comes in, washes his hands, and gives you the examination that you came to get. My question to you is, "Will you go back?" The answer is "yes." The reason you will go back again is because your natural health is important to you and you want to get rid of any kind of pain in your body. You cooperate with the doctor and the hospital because you understand that you are not your doctor's only patient. You know there are many others who are suffering in their bodies and trying to get well. You don't tell your doctor that you are mad at him because you came at 10 o'clock and it is currently 11 o'clock and you are just seeing him.

The same should be true when it comes to your spiritual life. There are times when due to the help people need, services linger. At our local church, we begin promptly every Sunday morning at 9:30 a.m. and we also have an 11 a.m. service. However, those who came to the 11 o'clock service a few years ago had to sometimes sit through the things that were carrying over from the 9:30 service. It was due to the fact that some of the members were facing challenges

Spiritual Upgrade

with cancer, debt, or some other marital situation. My wife and I were aware of many of these issues even though many visitors weren't. We would try to make those who showed up at 11'oclock feel as comfortable as possible, but the bottom line is getting people well. Today, many of these people are totally healed. Some who were in debt now own houses, and some have had their marriages totally restored. The carnal response would be, so what. If people come at 11 o'clock, you should start at that time, but let's look at this carefully. First of all, the service at 9:30 a.m. is important, and what the Holy Spirit is imparting should never be taken for granted. God, who makes all the final decisions, must be allowed to speak to his people because he has the solutions that we need.

There are times when two college basketball games or two NBA Games are scheduled to come on television. They tell you what time the first game starts and what time the second game starts. However, if the first game goes into triple overtime, the announcer states that he is going to stay right there with the game and will be with the second game shortly. You may not have any concern at all about the first game because you like the teams in the second game. Yet, the second game can't start until the first game ends because the announcer knows that even though you might not be interested, someone is. Sometimes we go into <u>spiritual overtime</u>, and we must be ready.

We have to consider others better than ourselves and desire to see them set free. Excellence can never be upgraded in the body of Christ if we make deliverance unimportant. Carnal minded men and women desire to rush in and rush out of the sanctuary, but those who understand real hurts and real pains of others will not care how long it takes as long as people get delivered. I remember when I was desiring to be filled with the Holy Ghost many years ago. One of the reasons I stopped trying to be filled that night was because I was concerned that it was taking too long. I thought in my mind these people are getting tired of me, and I had better stop trying tonight and try again another time. I remember walking back to the college campus that night with many fellow students feeling dejected when I was approached by one of the students with words that would forever change my life. Her name was Cathy Gamble. Cathy told me that she wanted me to be filled with the Holy Ghost. She said, "No matter how long it takes don't let anybody cause you to leave the altar if you truly want to be filled with the Spirit." She said that she along with some of the others would tarry there all night if they had to until I received the Spirit. Thank God for Cathy and saints like this. She was moving in the spirit of excellence.

Excellence also involves you and I using what we have at our disposal until God gives us more. This is why we shouldn't compare ourselves with others. We must remember that the goal is to demonstrate high quality or fineness where we are. This is why we go from glory to glory. None of us start out with the excellence that we will eventually find ourselves walking in. We must give it a continual upgrade. What looked like excellence at one stage in your life will not look like excellence at another stage in your life. As you grow and mature in your relationship with the Lord, you will be provoked by the grace of God, as well as others who love you, to <u>step it up</u>.

> "Happiness: the full use of your powers along the lines of excellence."
> **John F. Kennedy**

This famous quote made by our thirty fifth President should fuel the fire for excellence in our spirit. I believe until we fully use the power (strength and ability) on the inside of us with excellence we are going to be miserable. You have what it takes to be impressive. The work that you do will improve as you continue to work what you have right now. Don't say that you will start to do things with excellence when your ministry gets a certain amount of people. Start right where you are and work your way up.

> "We cannot do great deeds unless we are willing to do small things that make up the sum of greatness."
> **Theodore Roosevelt** (26th President)

You must know that your Heavenly Father made a deposit in you that will bring a great blessing to your community and nation. The power of God will release things through you that will make tremendous improvements in the lives of others. God will do this because he knows the most important commodity in the world today is man. We are the main focus in his sight. He longs to have us lifted up to high spiritual dimensions, so he can reveal more of himself to us. This desire to send out excellence to reach man is a must.

> "Man is still the most extraordinary computer of all."
> **John F. Kennedy** (35th President)

This type of spiritual upgrade in excellence will demand that you put aside small thinkers. It will cause you to step into new arenas of thought by brilliant men and women around you with a desire to see others rise up.

> "America demands and deserves big things from us—and nothing big ever came from being small."
> **Bill Clinton** (42nd President)

I can recall a particular Sunday morning at about 9:15, arriving at Newness of Life, the church that I pastor. That particular morning as I arrived, the service began promptly, and we were scheduled to start our 11 o'clock service when at about 10:55, a gentleman stepped in the door yelling and screaming. "She's gone Pastor Sharpe; she's gone. My baby left me this morning. It hurts so bad. She's gone Pastor Sharpe; she's gone." This young man wasn't a member of our church. He had grown up with me in the world before I got saved and was hurting so bad that he came to see me. We were about to start praise and worship service when all of this took place. He was weeping profusely and kneeled at my feet. I kneeled down

Spiritual Upgrade

with him and told him to take his time and explain what happened as I consoled him with a pat on the back. He apologized for disturbing our service but stated he didn't know where else to go that morning. When he woke up and tried to awaken a young lady who he had lived with for years, he discovered that she was dead. The ambulance had come and gotten her and took her body away, and now he was totally devastated. I began to minister to him and had prayer with him. It took a while as he openly explained his hurt to us as a church. This wasn't the time to try to rush this man in the back somewhere. This was the time for the church to see ministry in action. I know some who came at 11 o'clock weren't expecting this at all, but this is what Jesus is all about. I made an open appeal for him to accept Jesus as the Lord of his life, but he said he wasn't ready yet. However, several others accepted Jesus as the appeal was made. Notice a song wasn't sung or a message wasn't preached. The service hadn't started, but people were already being delivered.

I also saw some people to my surprise and amazement looking at their watches as if to say that they didn't come for this. They came to have a service, but they didn't understand that God's agenda is deliverance. He was glorified. Later, as time went by, this particular young man was working for a construction company that was renovating a building in the city. He saw me as I was about to go into the Post Office and called out to me with great joy. As he spoke to me, I noticed that they had ceiling tiles that they were about to be thrown away. They looked almost brand

Spiritual Upgrade

new. I asked him about them, and he told me that he would ask his boss. He assured me that if his boss said we could have them that he would deliver them to our church. Well, to make a long story short he delivered the tiles, and we used them to replace some tiles in our facility at that time. All of this happened because we valued people more than we did our watches. Let's be prompt and punctual, but let's also upgrade ourselves with this type of excellence.

Anybody who truly knows me will tell you that I don't believe in going to church late or being late when we minister out of town. I always give any church that I am called to go serve the utmost respect. I believe excellence is what our God and his kingdom is all about. I am just trying to get you to see that it is not excellence to strive to start on time and then leave before the benediction is over. I remember my brother and I were at a particular meeting in Raleigh. The guest speaker was Dr. Creflo Dollar. People showed up early to hear him minister the word at the RBC Center. He delivered a great message, but at the end when he was making the altar call for people to be filled with the Holy Ghost, people were leaving. My brother, Wayne and I were so saddened and grieved by this. We both wondered how can people who say they love the Lord begin to leave at this particular part of the service. Isn't this why Jesus came? This should be the very pulse of our being. We who are saved should be taking a posture of prayer while the altar call is being made. In spite of Dr. Dollar telling the people not to move or leave, people were still moving.

Spiritual Upgrade

My brother and I stayed, and we saw almost one hundred and fifty people come up to the altar that night to be filled with the Holy Ghost. We left there excited as the ushers escorted them to a particular place to be filled with the Spirit but at the same time we couldn't believe how people rushed to their cars at such a divine moment in the service. This isn't excellence. I am not saying what these people had to do the next day wasn't important. I am simply saying that seeing people get delivered from the authority of the devil and translated into the kingdom of God is more important.

Excellence shows respect to the manifestations of God. It states that whatever God is doing I want to see it and participate in it as well. You and I should delight in this and rejoice with people as they experience it. My brother and I reverenced that moment and begin to reminisce. We thought about the day we got saved and received the Holy Ghost. This is what should happen every time we see people walk the aisle to be born again. It should be an exciting time in our lives. We know that we are seeing God's work take place. It should be marvelous in our eyes.

We need an upgrade in excellence that will cause us to say, "The food place can wait. This is God's time." Others may leave, but you and I should function in excellence which means we can't do what everybody else does. We have to be <u>better</u>. We should say, "I am not leaving until God is finished!"

UPGRADING THROUGH THE TRUMPET

"The quality of American life must keep pace with the quantity of American goods. This country cannot afford to be materially rich and spiritually poor."
John F. Kennedy (35th President)

This is truly an astounding statement made by one of the greatest men that our country has ever known. He was a man who had enough insight to know that creating goods alone wouldn't be enough to make our nation great. We have to take a look at the spiritual side and monitor where we are with the Lord. Every true man and woman of God has to admit that we have lost something spiritually that has caused our nation to suffer. We have too many people trying to judge everything based on the material side and didn't see that we were being stripped spiritually. We need to hear the trumpet blow loud and clear to cause an awakening to take place in the body

Spiritual Upgrade

of Christ. We must look into the unseen world and expect the unseen to take authority over the seen. No matter how big our houses get or luxurious our cars are they are no substitute for seeking God's face.

The children of Israel weren't a spiritual minded nation. The only time they noticed that something was wrong with their spiritual condition was based upon natural losses. Once they saw natural losses then they would heed the voice of the prophets. I believe many great men and women of God have been inviting America to pray and fast, but because of the blessings and increase that we have seen throughout the past years, we haven't heeded the voice of the trumpet. People have been busy making all kinds of excuses as to why they couldn't come to church or pray. Yet, the natural conditions are deteriorating at such a pace that we must shift our attention to the spiritual arena for answers. God has always used bad times as a time of spiritual upgrade for his people. God is challenging every anointed vessel to train his people to stop looking at broken cisterns and look to him. It is our prayers that will turn this whole thing around. It is our desire to hunger and thirst after him like we have never sought him before that will move our economy. The President and those in authority need the prayers that we have to offer. If the prayers and fasting of Nineveh could turn their nation, you can't tell me that our prayers can't turn our nation. As we rend our hearts and not our garments, God will bring our nation to the top again.

The spiritual upgrade that this world so desperately needs will never take place without preachers (apostles, prophets, evangelists, pastors and teachers) and others lifting up their voices. We must blow the trumpet and sound the alarm.

Joel 2:1 *"Blow Ye the trumpet in Zion, and sound the alarm..."*

Notice according to this verse the trumpet must blow in Zion. The people who must listen are Zion or the church. God has always wanted his people to call out to him. He will respond to this nation when his people cry out to him. God loves us too much to let us go down, but we must acknowledge that we have moved from the place of calling on him. We are the people who should have an awareness that the only stable thing that we can trust is God.

We have a mandate upon our lives to cause people to know that when people pull away from God, we lose out. Yes, even in the natural we suffer tremendously when things are off spiritually. Things around us are eaten up, taken away from us, and ultimately destroyed. Our walk with God must be upgraded so God will leave a blessing behind.

Joel 2:14 *"Who knoweth if he will return and repent, and leave a blessing behind him; even a meat offering and a drink offering unto the Lord your God."*

It should be our desire to see God do great and marvelous things in our lives. However, we must be fully aware that God responds to the spiritual condition of our hearts. The trumpet helps us turn our hearts toward God. We begin to sanctify a fast, call a solemn assembly, and gather the people together to ask God to have his way among us.

Through the preaching of the word, we should understand that when our spiritual condition falters the country and nation will falter as well. God is ready to send us corn, wine, and oil so we can be satisfied. He is ready to drive away every army and foe that has been taking things away from us. God is ready to drive away every debt and bill in your life as long as you upgrade yourself spiritually. If we make the necessary changes in our spiritual walk with God, we don't have to fear. God will restore. He will send the rain. He will give us wheat. He will send overflow of wine and oil. God will cause us to eat in plenty and be satisfied. So blow preacher blow!

Joel 2:26 *"And ye shall eat in plenty, and be satisfied, and praise the name of the Lord your God, that hath dealt wondrously with you: and my people shall never be ashamed."*

EPILOGUE
(CHALLENGE YOURSELF)

There are many people who have been afforded the pleasure of seeing me grow into the man of God that I am today. I am in no ways finish or through manifesting Jesus Christ in my mortal body. However, I must admit without them admonishing me to pray, read the Bible, and fast, I wouldn't be as far as I am today. Many who listen to our radio broadcast and television broadcast will never fully comprehend how much their kind words exhorting us to continue to stay on the wall fully mean to me. Yet, their words only spark the fire on the inside of me to challenge myself. I continue to set new goals and dreams before myself that challenge me not to be satisfied. I believe the highest form of motivation is self-motivation.

"Things do not happen. Things are made to happen."
John F. Kennedy (35th President)

I so desperately want the words and ideas presented in this book to radically change your life. I want you to push yourself to make these upgrades in your life and refuse to be lukewarm. I no longer want you to wait until your pastor or some other great leader challenges your spirituality. I want you to arise and go after God like you never have before. I want you to understand that once you challenge yourself to a new spiritual upgrade, you will begin to experience inward victory and change like you've never experienced it before. People who challenge themselves perform and do things which cause others to marvel.

Challenge yourself to reach for the sacred things that will bring about a shift in your life and surroundings. I want you to challenge yourself this year to walk in spiritual authority and might. I want you to challenge yourself to win the lost. Challenge yourself to pray and fast. Challenge yourself to give at a whole new level. Challenge yourself to be friendly and loving to others. Challenge yourself to go to the House of God. Challenge yourself to be a blessing to everyone you come in contact with.

Genesis 12:1 (Amplified) says, *"Now [in Haran] the Lord said to Abram, Go for yourself [for your own advantage]"*

God in this verse is exhorting Abram to challenge himself to make spiritual and natural progress. He is letting Abram know that he can't afford to wait on everybody else. He has to make a move and make

Spiritual Upgrade

it now. You are reading this book because it's time to make a spiritual move. This move will be profitable to you first and then it will bless others. It will put you into strange or unfamiliar territory. The Holy Ghost wants you to heed his exhortation and save yourself from this untoward generation. God wanted Abram to know him in a whole new way and the only person that could stop this from happening would be him. He couldn't consider what his family and friends would think or say. This was personal.

It is so important that you understand the word I just used, personal. Your relationship with God will never take off or go to another level if you fail to make it a personal thing. We function and cooperate with the local church, but we must take our relationship with God as our personal responsibility. My spiritual walk with God has got to become important to me. I will never challenge myself if it is not. The day of just going through the motions must end for you. It must be about God and growing in him or it's about nothing. Your walk with God may not be esteemed by others, but it must be esteemed by you. I must not allow my relationship with God to grow cold, dry, or stale. I must keep it hot and on fire. I don't care what everybody else in the local assembly is doing. I must pursue God with my whole heart. I must place a constant demand on myself to eat the word of God and pray on a daily basis.

I remember my college days, when I went home for the summer, I challenged myself to grow. I knew when I returned back to college there would be new faces and new spiritual battles to fight. I knew that my spiritual growth would bring new victories. I stayed in the word and prayer as often as possible. I attended regularly scheduled Bible class and Sunday services. Everything that the man of God would preach or teach I would go home and study it some more. I committed the word of God to memory. It was alive in me and would flow out of me like water. When I returned to Shaw University from summer vacation, I was ready. I was armed and ready to advance the kingdom of God. I would see many believers hanging on the block, but I had become addicted to the word and prayer. Every spare moment became an opportunity to upgrade my personal relationship with the Lord. I challenged myself to be more and more like Jesus. Others began to notice that I had been with Jesus and many started to seek God for themselves. I learned that to seek God you have to become familiar with three powerful words. These three words revolutionized my life. They are Desire, Discipline, and Delight.

The order that I have placed these words is vital to the personal victory you will have. The first one is **Desire**. You will never grow beyond your desire for spiritual things. Your hunger is the thing that drives you and causes you to walk away from all hindrances. You must be desperate. You must have a desire for God that is greater than anything or anybody in the world. If your desire for him isn't strong enough, the devil will cheat you out of this powerful relationship with the Lord. My desire for God was so strong that I could hardly go to bed because I wanted to stay up all night reading and praying. I burned the midnight oil seeking God. I would sit at my desk in college reading praying and meditating. God tasted delicious, and I couldn't get enough of him. This desire still drives me today. I am still like a kid in a candy store. The Lord is so wonderful and spending time with him is so delightful. Let me warn you in advance concerning the criticism that you will receive. There will be those who know nothing about having a strong desire for God. They will accuse you of going overboard, but we live by our appetite. Some people can only eat one plate of food before they become full. Some need two or three plates of food before they are satisfied. The difference between the two is appetite or desire. My desire for God requires more and more each year. I challenge myself all the time in this area. I never compare my appetite to someone else's. I only keep tabs of where mine is with the Lord. You can never do this to brag because pride will bring us down. Your desire is controlled by your humility before God.

The second thing is ***Discipline***. It takes setting a time and place each day to meet with God. The same way you have a time to get up in the morning we need a time to be with God. I tell people all the time I don't know what time I will come out of prayer, but I do know what time I will start talking to him. Again, this is your own personal time. Don't choose what time is convenient for somebody else or allow anyone to bring you in bondage about the time you choose. God wants to meet with you. He's got something to tell you, and you've got something to tell him. Guard this time and you will find personal growth taking place in your life. This type of discipline is so good for you and me. God is waiting to fellowship with you. Don't allow the friends or family to cause you to dishonor this time. This is sanctified time. Many believers have a day and a time that their local church prays, but they fail to set a time that they pray alone with God. Real growth takes place in the time you spend alone with God. This is when your discipline will be tried. The phone will ring or maybe something you enjoy watching may come on television. You must have the discipline to push all that aside and talk to God. Also while you are alone you will have to fight to keep from going to sleep or allowing your mind to wander. Your mind will think about food or something that will get your thoughts off God. You will have to contend with the enemy and your flesh to win in this personal time with your heavenly Father. You will have to breakthrough these moments. If you don't, you will allow yourself to be brought out of your prayer closet too soon. The deep intimacy with the Lord will never be a reality for you unless you are disciplined. You can't afford to lose here. Challenge yourself to have the discipline to call your mind to a renewed focus on God. There is too much at stake.

The third and final thing you must challenge yourself with is ***Delight***. There will come a moment in the intimate moments with God that prayer will become a rightful thing for you. It will become fun. It will shift from work to fun. This is the place that the devil never wanted you to experience. He was trying to discourage you from getting to the delightful stage.

Spiritual Upgrade

This is when prayer gets so good you will feel like never quitting. The prayer language and interpretations are coming and the glory of God is in the room with you. All you see is the Lord, who is high and lifted up. Time is no longer an issue. Your mind isn't thinking about anyone else but God. He has taken over your whole being. You start uttering things to him that only a person totally consumed or lost in love would say. All you can do is tell him how much you love and appreciate him. Yes, you said some of these things earlier in your prayer, but it is totally different now. The words are more intense and meaningful to you. They are coming out of the mouth of a man or woman who is looking at their God from a whole new perspective. Two lovers are involved in a bliss beyond human understanding. This delightful stage is the thing that will cause you to return. This is the place where your spiritual senses are heightened. This is the place where you start to hear words that everybody won't understand. Only those who have been there can explain or understand this. You're in the place where the voice of God has you captivated. You feel like you just got saved. You feel like you and God just got married. It is glorious! You're caught up! This is when you finish seeking him that you need to read your Bible. The word at this moment leaps off the pages. It has so much life. You are now ready to face and defeat anything that tries to stand in your way.

Again let me remind you that nobody gets to this place if they don't challenge themselves. I can only tell you about this wonderful place. It is your Eden,

Spiritual Upgrade

but you will never experience it if you refuse to challenge yourself. You will have to push some things aside and make some serious adjustments in many areas of your life, but you won't regret it. You will become a giant in spiritual things. The dimension of the spirit that you will begin to walk in will amaze you and others. You will be very open to God. When God speaks, you will show no signs of hesitation. You will move immediately because your spiritual ear is open to his voice. You have become more alive to God than you have ever been in your entire life. Your personal awareness of him is keen. This is the level that you must challenge yourself to move to.

In other words, you must challenge yourself to be a Spiritual Giant. This spiritual upgrade that will manifest in your life will bring great pleasure to the heart of those who know you. They will know that you have more than some religious ritual, but instead you have an intimacy with the Lord that is becoming more intense as the days go by. They will know that you didn't arrive at this place just because you go to church. They have been to the same services that you have. They have attended the same revivals and conferences as you have. The difference is that you went home and stirred yourself to be alone with God. You did something they didn't. You pushed yourself to improve. You told yourself that there was more. You haven't grown content with where you are. No church or denomination can take credit for this. You gave yourself a personal challenge, and you kept it. The good news is that you're not through yet, continue to **CHALLENGE YOURSELF!**